Matthew Hale

Of the Nature of True Religion, the Causes of its Corruption, and

the Churches Calamity

Matthew Hale

Of the Nature of True Religion, the Causes of its Corruption, and the Churches Calamity

ISBN/EAN: 9783743419827

Manufactured in Europe, USA, Canada, Australia, Japa

Cover: Foto ©Lupo / pixelio.de

Manufactured and distributed by brebook publishing software
(www.brebook.com)

Matthew Hale

Of the Nature of True Religion, the Causes of its Corruption, and

the Churches Calamity

The Judgment of the late

LORD CHIEF JUSTICE
Sir Matthew Hale,

Of the Nature of

TRUE RELIGION,
THE
CAUSES of its CORRUPTION,

●And the *Churches Calamity*, by Mens

ADDITIONS and VIOLENCES:
With the defired Cure.

In three Difcourfes, written by himfelf at feveral times.

Humbly Dedicated to the Honourable Judges and Learned Lawyers, who knew and honoured the Author, becaufe in their
true Sentiments of Religion, and its Depravations, and the
Cure, the wellfare of *England*, under his Majefty, as well
as their own, is eminently concerned.

By the faithful Publifher, *RICHARD BAXTER.*

To which is annexed the Judgment of Sir *Francis Bacon* Lord
Verulam(St. *Albans*) and Chancellour of *England:* And fome-
what of Dr. *Ifaack Barrow's* on the fame fubject.

Mat. 5. 9. *Bleffed are the Peace-makers; for they fhall be called the Children of God.*
Rom. 14 17, 18. *The Kingdom of God is not meat and drink: but righteoufnefs and
peace, and joy in the holy ghoft. For he that in thefe things ferveth Chrift, is acceptable to God, and approved of men.*

LONDON, Printed for *B. Simmons* at the three Cocks near
the Weft-end of S. *Paul's* Church. 1684.

A
PREFACE,
With some Notes on these Discourses by the Publisher.

THe Publishing of these Discourses sheweth the great mutability of such weak understandings as my own : Till very lately no Price could have hired me to Publish them, lest it were a Violation of his Testament, which saith that he [would have no Writings of his Published, but what in his Life Time he gave to be Published] ; And he delivered not these in his Life Time to me. In my ignorance this satisfied me. But lately opening the Case to some Lawyers of known Eminence, Honour, and Integrity, they have convinced me that I cross his Will, and the Common good, by my Suppressing them.

The Case is this : When he was gone from us in great Weakness to the Place of his Death, in my last Letter to him, I told him how much good the Lord Bacon's Book called Considerations of Matters Ecclesiastical had done, with many that too justly suspect Clergy Contenders of Partiality ; and that the Honour and Just Esteem that God had given him with all sorts of Men he owed to the Service of him that gave it :
And

The Preface to the Reader.

And therefore knowing the doleful Case of this Land, as di ℈
*vided and striving about Religion, I intreated him that he
would Write his Judgment briefly and freely of the Cause and
Cure : The rather because his Contemplations were so acceptable to many.*

*In his last Letter answering this, He professeth that those
Contemplations were Printed without his Purpose, Knowledge,
or Consent, but thanks God if they did good, though beyond
his intent. But though the rest be full of kindness; I will not
Publish it, lest really it should violate his Will. But when he
was dead, he who Published his Contemplations; shewed me a
Bag of his Mannuscripts, small occasional Tractates, and gave
me out these three, saying, that They were directed [For Mr.
Baxter] By which I knew they were by him given me in answer
to my foresaid Letter, which Craved the Publication of his
Judgment of our Divisions. But I conjecture they had been
long before written by him at several Times, and much to the
same purpose ; and so I suppose that he gave them me, and left
the use of them to my Discretion. Now say these Learned
Lawyers, "A man may have several Wills in Writing in re-
"ference to several Things, not repugnant but consistent, and
"all shall stand and be taken as his last Will, and may make se-
"veral Executors, and give them several distinct Powers. And
"clausula generalis non porrigitur ad ea quæ Specialiter
"nominantur, And this Direction to you on that Occasion,
"maketh it a Legacy bequeathed to you : And the answering
"your Letter by it sheweth to what use : And his after like-
"ing of the publishing his Contemplations, sheweth that he
"was not utterly against appearing in Print.*

*By this and much more they Satisfie me, that it was my
Ignorance that made me resolve to Conceal them.*

*I confess the Deliverer thought it best for me to make one
Treatise out of them all, Because being not intended for Publication at the Writing of them, the same thing is repeated,*
                                                    especially

The Preface to the Reader.

especially in two of them. And that Repetition and the Bre-
vity made me long undervalue them.

But I take it as an intollerable piaculum *to put any alte-*
ring hand of mine to the Writings of such a Man; which I
profess I have not done in adding, expunging, or changing one
Word (save some false spelling of the Scribe: for only the La-
tin Verses, and an interlining or two, are his own hand; which
I know by many a Sheet that I have had from him.)

And as long as the Occasion of the Writing them is known,
I think it no dishonour to them to have these Repetitions: *At*
least not so much as my alterations would be: Yea it is use-
ful; first, as fully shewing the Readers, that these are no
hasty crude conceptions, but matters that long and deeply
dwelt in his heart. 2. And Great matters, *specially to* dull
or unwilling, *or* negligent *Readers or hearers, must be* oft repeated; *for a Transient touch passeth away from such without*
any Effect. O that the matter of these three Papers were
Written and spoken an hundred times, if it would make Ru-
lers, and Teachers, and People once truly to consider and receive
them as they deserve.

Yet upon oft perusal I find that the Repetition is joyned
with variety of inference and Application: And he hath too
Queasy a Stomach that will Nauseate them in so short dis-
courses on so great a Subject, so necessary to a People dissolving
by wilfull Divisions, by the delusion of Abaddon that is com-
monly Painted with a Cloven Foot.

I shall add the Contents for the Readers help. But I shall
not presume to animadvert on the matter, save in these few
Notes.

1. *Tract.* 1. pag. 4. *I suppose by* [Common assistances]
he meaneth not that which All men have: *But which is not*
Miraculous, *and all that rightly seek may hope for.*

P. 7. *Some of the Controversies which he Judged unde-*
terminable, I have Cause to think he at least came nearer

to

Ib. Among the Points not diſtinctly knowable without more Revelation than we yet have of it, *one is* [what is the Real Conſequence of the Baptiſm of Infants or its Omiſſion]. *But the Act of Uniformity Ejected all the Miniſters of* England, *that would not publickly, declare that they* Aſſent and Conſent, *that* [It is CERTAIN *BY THE WORD* of God, that Infants baptized, dying before actual Sin, are *UNDOUBTEDLY ſaved*] (*none excepted*). *Had the Convocation but cited that* Word of God *that ſaith this, this Good man might have been kept from taking that as* unknowable, *which every Conforming 'Miniſter in the Church is* Certain of, as an undoubted Article of Faith. *And it would have been a great kindneſs to the ſilenced Miniſters.*

Pag. 11. *His preference of Epiſcopacy before all other Governments, was his real Judgment. But it was its* Eſſentials *and not all the* Additionals *that he meant. For to my knowledge he would have been glad of the* Primitive Model · *of* Biſhop Uſher, (*Who was his much valued friend*).

In the 3d. Tract. *Pag.* 17. *the Scribe left an* A———— *for a word omitted, and I durſt not ſupply it by Conjecture.*

Who the Authors are that he ſo much blameth, ſpecially the Dialogiſt, *few will doubt, but I will not name, becauſe by the Report of his good Preaching and Life, I cannot but hope that he Repenteth of it.*

There is one S T. *that in an Invective againſt the* Proteſtant Reconciler (*a Book like this*) *and againſt* Dr. Stillingfleet, *inſinuates that I am not to be believed in my Report elſewhere given of Judge* Hales *words, that* [A new Act of Uniformity muſt heal *England,* &c. *In theſe three Treatiſes this incredulous man may ſee much more than that, which may expugne his Unbelief: And leſt any accuſe me of Forge-*
ry,

The Preface to the Reader.

ry, I hope to preserve the Manuscripts, and doubt not but the Lady Hale or Mr. Stevens hath a Copy of them. And because this Reverend Enemy to the Reconciler, (pleading for their Excommunication) was a Son of a Reverend Nonconformist (deceased) and lived sometime with me, at Kiderminster, and frequently walkt with me, and therefore may be thought to have known my incredibility; I ask him, why in all that time, [if he knew me to be a Lyar] would he never once tell me of it.

I take [Cursed be the Trimmers] and [Blessed are the Peace-makers] for direct contraries: And Christ to be Wiser and more credible than all the Enemies of Peace.

R. B.

THE

THE

CONTENTS

Of the firſt Diſcourſe.

The Contents.

The Contents of the Second Discourse.

a   *they*

The Contents.

The Contents of the third Discourse.

WHat the Christian Religion is, and what men true Christians are. p. 1 But many Additions in all ages have been made to it, by divers sorts, for divers designes and ends. Some by the authority of great Names, some by insensible gradations, some by supposed Congruity, some as for Order and Decency, some for discrimination of Parties, some for Political Ends, emergent occasions, Civil or Ecclesiastical Sanctions, &c. And the greatest Fervor and Animosity of men commonly laid out on these additions, by some for them, by others against them.

The unhappy Consequents.   p. 4.

1. Diversion from the true nature and use of Religion, by Zeal for entire Conformity to these additions or against them.

2. And so the Fervour of mens Spirits. let out the wrong way. p. 5.

3. Hence come Schisms and Factions, and Personal Animosities, discriminations, Censoriousness, estrangedness by ill advancing these opinions and little things.

4. The Bond of Charity broken, Severity, Persecution, Implacableness, endeavouring to supplant and disgrace Dissenters, worse scorns, reproach and vilifying than between Christians and Turks.   p, 6.

5. Increase

The Contents.

The

l.

The Contents.

The Contents of the Additional Testimonies.

1 THe Lord Bacons *words in his Advertisement of the Controversies of the Church of England.* 2. *His words in his Considerations for better Pacification and Edification of the Church of* England (*Lest the Reader accuse me of omitting any part, I had rather he would read all those two Treatises himself, than those Scraps*) 3 *Animadversions of the Transcriber.* 4. *Some passages of Doctor* Isaack Barrow.

OF

O F
RELIGION.

The Ends and Uses of it, and the Errors of Men touching it.

TRUE Religion is the greatest *Improvement, Advantage,* and *Priviledge* of *Humane Nature* ; and that which gives it the noblest and highest Pre-eminence above other visible Creatures.

We may observe in many Bruit Beasts and Birds admirable Instincts, Dexterities, and Sagacities; and in some of them some dark resemblances of Reason, or Ratiocination : But *Religion* is so *appropriate* to the *Humane Nature,* that there are scarce any sort of Men, but have *some Religion* : Nor do the most subtle or sagacious Bruits afford any signs thereof, as communicated to their Natures.

It is one of the chiefest Mercies and Blessings that Almighty God hath afforded to the Children of Men, and that which signally manifests his Providential Care towards

B
wards

wards and over them, that in all Ages and among all Na-
tions he hath given to them *some Means* and *Helps* to dif-
cover unto them, though in different Degrees, some
principal Sentiments of true Religion: 1. By the secret
Characters, and *Impressions,* and Structures thereof in their
Minds and *Consciences.* 2. By his *Glorious* and admirable
Works, commonly called the *Works of Nature.* 3. By
signal *Providences,* and *Providential Regiment* of the
World. 4. By raising up *Men* in all Ages of *great Wisdom,*
Observation, and *Learning,* which did instruct the more
ignorant in this great Concernment, the Rudiments of Natural Religion. 5. By *Traditionary* Transmission of many
important Truths and Directions of Life, from Ancestors
to their Posterity, and others: Though in process of time
evil Customs and evil Men did in a great measure impair
and corrupt the Sentiments and Practices of Men, notwithstanding these helps. Therefore the same Mercy and
Goodness of God, for the preservation and propagation of
the true Religion, was pleased to substitute a more fixed
and permanent means; namely, the *Holy Scriptures,* or
Divine Revelations, committed to Writing in the Books of
the Old and New Testament. Though the Religion delivered in both Testaments, be in substance the same; yet
the true Religion was more fully, and plainly, and distinctly
delivered by Christ and his Apostles in the New Testament,
together also with some additional Instructions, for the
better preservation and propagation thereof to Mankind,
and divers additional Evidences to prove and manifest the
truth of this Religion, to procure its belief and accepta-
tion: As the *Birth,* *Miracles,* *Death,* *Resurrection,* and
Ascension of Christ Jesus, the great Reformer of the *Jewish,*
and great Institutor of the Christian Religion, so called from
Christ that taught and asserted it. The Christian Religion is the most perfect Rule of our Duty to God, our selves,
and

and others ; and was defigned principally for thefe Great Ends.

1. To *reſtore* to the Glorious *God*, the *Honour, Duty,* and *Obedience* of his Creature, Man ; teaching him to Know, to Glorifie and Serve his Creator, to be Thankful to him, to ſubmit to his Will, to obey his Law and Command , to be thankful for his Mercies, to acknowledge him in all his ways, to call upon him, to Worſhip him , to depend upon him, to walk ſincerely in his fight, to admire and adore his Greatneſs and Goodneſs in all his works, eſpecially in the great work of the Redemption of Mankind by his Son Chriſt Jeſus.

2. To inable *Man* to attain *everlaſting Happineſs*, the perpetual Viſion of the Glorious God, and to fit and prepare him to be a partaker of the Inheritance of the Saints in Light and Glory.

3. To compoſe and ſettle Mankind in ſuch a decent and becoming rectitude, order, and deportment in this World, as may be ſuitable to the Exiſtence of a Reaſonable Nature, and the Good of Mankind : Which conſiſts principally in a double relation: 1. To a *Mans ſelf, Sobriety.* 2. To *others,* which conſiſts in thoſe two great Habits or Diſpoſitions beneficent to Mankind , *viz. Righteouſneſs,* or *Juſtice* and *Charity,* or *Love* and *Beneficence.*

Theſe three Great Ends are ſuccinctly delivered, *Tit.* 2. 11, 12. For *the Grace of God, that bringeth Salvation hath appeared unto all men, teaching us, that denying ungodlineſs and worldly luſts, we ſhould live Soberly, Righteouſly, and Godly in this preſent World.* Here we have theſe three Ends of Chriſtian Religion. 1. *Godlineſs,* or our Duty to God. 2. Salvation, or our own everlaſting Happineſs. 3. *Sobriety, Righteouſneſs,* which alſo includeth *Charity,* a part of Evangelical Righteouſneſs.

And becauſe Chriſtian Religion was intended and inſtituted

tuted for the good of Man-kind, whether Poor or Rich, Learned or Unlearned, Simple or Prudent, Wife or Weak, it was fitted with fuch *plain, eafie*, and *evident* Directions, both for things to be *known*, and things to be *done*, in order to the attainment of the End for which it was defigned, that might be underftood by any Capacity, that had the ordinary and common ufe of Reafon or Humane Underftanding, and by the common affiftance of the Divine Grace might be practifed by them.

The *Credenda*, or things to be known or believed, as fimply neceffary to thofe Ends, are but few, and intelligible, briefly delivered in that Summary of Chriftian Religion, ufually called the *Apoftles Creed*.

The *Agenda*, or things to be *done* or *forborn*, are thofe few and excellent Precepts, delivered by Chrift and his Apoftles, in that *little Book* of the *New Teftament*; and yet even the tenth part of that little Book will contain all the Precepts of Chriftian Duty and Obedience contained in that Book: And in brief the *Baptifmal Covenant*, as it is contained in the Liturgy, and Explanation thereof in the Church Catechifm ufed among us, together with the Precepts of the Decalogue, contain in effect a Summary or brief Epitome of our Chriftian Duty.

And certainly it was neceffary and becoming the Wifdom of the moft Wife God, that that Religion and Doctrine, which equally concerned Men of all Kinds and Capacities, fhould be accordingly accommodated, as might be ufeful for all. If the Doctrine or Precepts of Chriftian Religion fhould have been delivered in over fublime or feraphical expreffions, in high Rhetorical Raptures, in intricate and fubtile Phrafes or Stile, or if it fhould have been furcharged with multitude of particulars, it would have been like a Sealed Book, to the far greateft part of Mankind, who yet were equally concerned in the Bufinefs and End

of

of Religion, with the greateſt Philoſophers and Clerks in the World.

Upon what hath been ſaid, we may therefore Conclude,

1. That there is not, nor indeed may not be any great difficulty in the attaining of a *true ſaving Knowledge* of Chriſtian Religion.

2. That the Duties of Chriſtian Religion are not of ſo vaſt an Extent, but the Knowledge of them may be alſo attained by an Ordinary Capacity *willing to Learn.*

3. That Conſidering that God Almighty is never wanting with his Grace to. Aſſiſt thoſe that ſincerely endeavour and Deſire to Obey him and Serve him, it is not ſo Difficult a Buſineſs to perform an Evangelical Obedience to the Precepts of the Goſpel, I ſay an *Evangelical Obedience*, though not a *Perfect Obedience*; an Obedience that is *Sincere*, though many times *Weak*, and failings, which nevertheleſs are forgiven, and their Sincere though Imperfect Obedience accepted by Almighty God through the Merits and Interceſſion of Chriſt, and our own Humiliation and ſincere Repentance for our failings. ᵃ

And, 4. That when all is done, in *this Belief* and *this Obedience* Conſiſts our *Chriſtian Religion*. This is the One thing *Neceſſary*, the *Magnum Oportet*, which is of higheſt Concernment and greateſt Importance to Mankind.

But now if we do but look about us in the World, and obſerve and conſider the Matters, wherein Men for the *moſt part* do place, *Religion* we ſhall find quite another kind of Rate and Nature of Religion than what Chriſt Inſtituted or intended, and yet all vailed and ſhrowded under the Name of *Chriſtian Religion*; and greater weight and ſtreſs laid upon them than upon the *True, Real, grand Imports* of Chriſtian Religion.

1. I ſhall begin with the Subtilties of great Scholars, Schoolmen, and Scholaſtick Divines. Theſe have turned
Chriſti-

Chriftian Religion into a moft Curious and difficult Specu-
lation, and that which was defigned by Chrift Jefus as a plain
Direction to every Capacity, to be a Guide to a Righteous,
Holy, and Sober Life here; and to attain Everlafting Life
hereafter, they have [made] a meer *exercife of* Wit, and a
Piece of greater fubtilty than the abftrufeft Philofophy or
Metaphyficks. And this they have done principally
thefe ways :

1. By *Difputes* about Queftions, that, as they are not
in themfelves *Neceffary* to be known, fo they are in their
own Nature Impoffible for Humane Underftandings to
determine : As for inftance ; many, if not all, the Points
controverted between the *Arminians* and *Calvinifts,* as touching the *manner of the Decrees of God,* what kind of *Influence* he hath *upon the Wills of men.* The *manner of* the
Divine Knowledge of things Future, Contingent, or *Poffible.*
The *Refiftability* or *Irrififtability* of Divine *Grace.* The *Nature of Eternity,* and *Infinitude,* and *Indivifibility.* The
manner of the *Exiftence of* the *Three Perfons* in the *Unity* of
Effence. The *Nature of Angels* and *Spirits* ; the *Manner* and
Degrees, and *Method* of their *knowledge of things* ; their feveral *Ranks and Orders* ; and infinite more Speculations and
Difputes of things that do not in their own Nature fall under the difcovery of a Humane Underftanding, by the ordinary Courfe of Ratiocination, and are impoffible to be
known further than they are diftinctly revealed by Almighty God, and as it were induftrioufly kept Secret by
Almighty God, becaufe they are not of ufe to Mankind to be
known. It is far more poffible for a Child of three years
old to have a true Conception of the moft abftrufe Points
in Philofophy, or in the Myftical Reafons of State or Politick Government of a Kingdom, than for the Wifeft man
that ever was, without Revelation from God, to have any
tollerable Conception or Notion of things of this Nature
with any tollerable Certainty or Evidence.   2. Again

2. Again there are other Points difputed which are of a *lower* allay, and yet not to be diftinctly known without more *clear* Revelation than we yet have of it, nor yet of any *Neceffity* for us *diftinctly* to know: As for inftance, Concerning the *Nature and Manner* of *Tranfmiffion of Original Sin*; *How far* the fins of *immediate or remote Parents* affect their *Pofterity* with *Guilt or Punifhment* ; The *Origination* of the *Humane Soul*; How far the Efficacy of the *Sacrifice of Chrift was intentionally for all Men* ;Concerning, the *Means of Communication thereof to Infants, Ideots, and the invinfible Ignorant*; What is the *real Confequence of* 👉 *Baptifm of Infants,* or its *Omiffion*; How far the *Will of man* is *Operative* to his *Converfion*, or *Perfeverance*; Wherein the *formal* Nature of *Juftification* Confifts; How far forth *Faith fingly* is fufficient for it, without *Sanctification* and *Habitual Holinefs* at laft, and how far forth the *Sincere Love of God* by a perfon invinfibly ignorant of many or moft Points of Chriftian Religion is *fufficient* thereunto; Concerning the *Eftate of the feparate Soul* before the *laft Judgment*, and how far it enjoys the *Beatifical* Vifion before the *Refurrection*.

Difputes touching thefe and the like difficult Queftions, have blown up mens Fancies with Speculations, inftead, of filling their Hearts with the true and genuine Effects of Chriftian Religion.

It is true, that Phyficians and Naturalifts do and may make Inquiries into the Method and Progrefs of *Generation*, and *Digeftion*, and *Sanguification*, and the motions of the *Chile*, the *Blood*, the *Humours*: For, 1. They have means of accefs to the difcovery thereof by Diffection and Obfervation. And, 2. It is of fome ufe to them in their Science, and the Exercife thereof. But when all is done, a man of a found Conftitution digefts his Meat, and his Blood Circulates, and his feveral Veffels and Intrails perform their offices, though

he

he know not diftinctly the Methods of their Motions and Operations. But thefe Speculations above-mentioned, in Points of Divinity, as they are not poffible to be diftinctly determined with any certainty, fo they are of little ufe to be known.

If the heart be feafoned with the true knowledge of the things that are revealed, and with the Life of the Chriftian Religion, and the love of God, it will be effectual enough to order his Life, and bring him to Everlafting Happinefs, though he be not, like an exquifite Anatomift, acquainted with a diftinct Comprehenfion or Knowledge of the feveral difficult Inquiries of this Nature. Believe what is required by the Word of God to be believed, and do your Duty, as by that Word is directed; fo that the Life of Religion, and the love of God be once fet on foot in the Soul, and there nourifhed, and commit your felf to the Faithfulnefs and Goodnefs of God, and this will be effectual to the great End of Religion, though all thefe Difputes be laid afide.

3. Again, A Third mifchief of *Scholafticks*, is in relation to *Practicks* : 1. Some *Cafuiftical Divines* have fo diftinguifhed concerning Religious External Duties, that they have left little Practical Religion or Morality in the World, and by their fubtle curious Diftinctions, have made almoft every thing Lawful, and with the *Pharifees*, in the time of our Saviour, have made void the Laws of God, (and of Man alfo) by their Traditions and Diftinctions: So that Religion towards God, and all Righteoufnefs and Sobriety, is fo thin and narrow, and fubtile, that by their Doctrine of *Probability*, and *Cafuiftical Diftinctions*, all the Bones thereof are loofned. It would be too long to give Inftances in particular: The late Velitations in *France* between fome of the Popifh Priefts and Jefuites furnifh the World with inftances enough of this kind.

2. The

2. The Second Inſtance is this, *The turning of the greateſt part of Religion into Politick Contrivances,* for attaining or upholding *Power, Wealth, or Intereſt.*

There have been Inſtances many in this kind among Secular Princes and States. This was the act of *Jeroboam* to ſet up Idolatrous Religion in *Samaria,* for preventing a return of the Ten Tribes to the Houſe of *David.* And we may obſerve it in moſt of the Religion eſtabliſhed by Heatheniſh Princes, which was ſo ordered to accomodate their Intereſt, though to the extreme corrupting of Natural Religion.

But there is not ſo eminent an Inſtance thereof in the whole World, as that of the *Ecelefiaſtical State of the Church of Rome,* who have corrupted, as much as in them lies, the moſt pure and innocent Religion that ever the world knew, namely, the Chriſtian Religion, by diſtorting it to Ends of *Wealth and Power,* and appendicating to it certain new *Doctrines* and *Practices* meerly to thoſe Ends. And not only ſo, but have laid the greateſt *weight* of *Religion* in the Obſervation of theſe *Politick Appendicatims* ; ſo that a man, that either queſtions or not obſerves theſe *Politick Additaments,* runs as ſevere a Cenſure and Danger among them, as he that denies the moſt unqueſtionablePrinciples of Chriſtian Religion. Such are their Doctrines of the *Popes Supremacy,* the *Popes Infallibility* ; the *neceſſity to Salvation* to be of the *Romiſh Church,* the *Adoration of* Images, Saints *departed,* and *Angels*; the *Veneration* of Reliques ; the Doctrine of *Purgatory, Indulgences,* and the *Church Treaſury* of *redundant Merits* ;the Doctrine and Practice of *Diſpenſations* and Indulgences; their *Canonization* of *Saints* ; their *Pilgrimages, numerous Ceremonies, Theatrical Spectacles* ; their Doctrine of *Tranſubſtantiation,* and divers other Superadditions and Appendications to Chriſtian Religion,which any perſon, not captivated by them, may with half an eye perceive

ceive

ceive to be invented and continued meerly for the support of the Grandure of an Univerfal Monarchy, which they mifcall *The Church*, and for the amaffing of *Wealth and Power* for the fupport of it, as might moft eafily be evinced by the particular Examination of all thofe Politick Appendixes.

And yet let any man obferve it, he fhall find as great a fervour for the upholding of thefe Doctrines and Practices, and as great a *jealoufie* of the leaft breach made upon them, as if the whole Concern of Chriftian Religion, and the Salvation of Souls lay in their Belief and Obfervance.

3. The third Inftance is in relation to the *Forms* of *Church Government* and *Ceremonies*. That *Ecclefiaftical Government* is neceffary for the prefervation of Religion, is evident to any reafonable and confiderate man: and that the *Epifcopal* Government conftituted in *England*, is a moft excellent Form of Ecclefiaftical Government, and exceeds all other Forms of Ecclefiaftical Government, may be eafily evinced ; and that it is the beft adapted to the Civil Government in this Kingdom, is vifible to any intelligent perfon: And yet I do not think that the Effence of Chriftian Religion Confifts in *this* or any *other particular Form* of *Government*. It is a great help to the prefervation of it in its Purity and Unity, and may be well called *Sepimentum Religionis Chriftianæ*, as the *Jews* call their Oral Traditions *Sepimentum Legis*, the Fence of the Law. But a man may be a *good and excellent Chriftian* under *this* or any *other Form* of Ecclefiaftical Government, nay in fuch places where poffibly there is no fettled Form of Ecclefiaftical Government eftablifhed.

But if we obferve many perfons in the world, we fhall find fome fo highly devoted to *this or that* particular *Form of Government*, as if all *the weight* of Chriftian Religion lay in it : Though the wife and fober fort of Conformifts know

and

and profefs this, yet there be fome rafh people that will prefently Un-church all the Reformed Churches beyond the Seas which are not under *Epifcopal Government*. That if they fee a man, otherwife of *Orthodox Principles*, of a *Pious* and *Religious* life, yet if *fcrupling fome Points* of *Ecclefiaſtical Government*, though peaceable, they will efteem him little better than a *Heathen or Publican*, a *Schifmatick*, *Heretick*, and what not: On the other fide, if they fee a man of great fervour in afferting the *Ecclefiaftical Government*, obfervant of *External Ceremonies*, though otherwife of a *loofe and diffolute life*, yet they will be ready to applaud him with the Stile of a *Son of the Church*, and upon that account over-look the Mifcarriages of his life, as if the Effence and Life of Chriftian Religion lay in the bare afferting of the beft Form of Ecclefiaftical Government.

On the other fide, there is as great an Extremity of the other hand: there are many indifcreet perfons, as well Divines as others, that having either by their *Education*, or by *Converfation* with Diffenters, or poffibly to gain a Party, taken upon them the Patronage or Afferting of fome other Form of Church-Government, either *Presbyterian* or *Independant*, or fome thing fram'd by their own invention, prefently cry down the Eftablifhed Government of the Church, as Antichriftian or Popifh, and cry up that which they have thus efpoufed as the only true Chriftian Regiment inftituted by Chrift; and prefently among them, and their Followers, this is made the difcriminative Mark of a True Chriftian. If they fee a man Conformable to the Eftablifhed Government, tho' he be pious, fober, and truly Religious, yet they defpife and neglect him, cenfure him as a Formalift, and without the Power of Godlinefs: But if a man will but *revile* the Eftablifhed Government, and be *bold* againft it, cry it down, and cry up the New Inftitution into which they are lifted, tho' the man be Covetous,

Un-

Uncharitable, Hard-hearted, Proud, Impetuous, and poffibly otherwife Loofe in his Converfation, yet fuch a man
fhall be cherifhed, applauded, and cryed up for a Saint, a Precious Man, and Zealous for the Truth.

And although *Decent Ceremonies*, that are for the Prefervation of the Dignity of Religion, and to keep due Order and Regularity, are not Effential Parts of Chriftianity,
nor were ever fo efteemed by wife and fober men, and yet
are of ufe and convenience in the Church, neverthelefs, we
may eafily obferve among men the fame Extremes as are
before noted : fome placing the whole *weight* of Religion
in their *ftrict Obfervance*, and making them the *principal*,
if not the *only Badge of a Son of the Church*, *hateing* and
defpifing thofe that *fcruple any thing* in them, or that do
not come up in *every punctilio* to their Obfervance, though
they be otherwife *found* in the Principles of Faith, *pious* and
ftrict in their lives, *juft* and *honeft* to all men, and fober,
temperate and blamelefs.

On the other fide, there be a fort of men that place
the greateft ftrefs and difcriminating Point of Chriftian
Religion in *oppofing* and *decrying* all *Inftituted Ceremonies*,
though *Innocent*, *Decent*, and without any the leaft touch
of Superftition in them, yet thefe muft be decried as Popifh, Antichriftian, deftructive of Chriftian Liberty, and
the Party that with moft boldnefs and vehemence declaims
againft them, is valued by them as a moft precious man, a
man of zeal and courage, and needs little elfe to juftifie
and magnifie him with his Party.

On the other fide, though a man be of an holy and confcientious life, found in Principles, fober, blamelefs, peaceable ; yet if he obferve thefe blamelefs Ceremonies,
though with great moderation and Charity to Diffenters,
he fhall be flighted and undervalued, efteemed a Formalift,
a Time-ferver, or at beft, a man wanting Courage, Zeal,
Lukewarm,

Lukewarm, Timorous, and wanting the Power of Godli-
nefs.Such wild and wrong Meafures do men of Extremes on
all hands take of the true Effence and Ends of Chriftianity.

4. Again, even among Profeffors of the Proteftant
Religion, there are divers difputed and Controverted
Points; as between the *Calvinifts* and *Arminians,* efpecially touching the *Univerfality* of the *Redemption* by Chrift,
Perfeverance and *Falling from Grace*; and almoft every day
there arife certain *new Opinions,* fome of *greater* importance,
but very commonly of *fmall* and incnofiderable moment;and
thefe are taken up by the feveral Parties poffibly agreeing in
the fame Fundamentals of Chriftian Religion. And fome
times they are entertained by a Party of men, becaufe
their Paftors are of that Opinion, or feem to be fo; though
often they are taken up,or inftilled into a Party, to make a
difcriminative Mark between Perfons of feveral Congrega-
tions. And then it is wonderful to fee with what fervour
each Party maintains his Tenent, and as great weight is laid
upon it, as if the whole ftrefs of Chriftian Religion, and
the Salvation of the Souls of men lay upon it; when God
knows they are not of any moment in it.

Such was the old Controverfie between the *Eaftern* and
Weftern Churches about *Eafter-day,* and ancienter than
that, in the Apoftles times, about *Eating of meats offered
to Idols,* and among us at this day touching the five *Arminian* Queftions. And yet we fhall fee men as fervent and
zealous about them, as cenforious of Diffenters from them,
as fond of thofe of the fame Opinion with them, as if all
the Articles of the Chriftian Faith were immediately concerned in them; when all the while they are not of
any moment to the Salvation of men, nor of any concernment to the Chriftian Religion, or the Ends thereof, but
are only Artifices impofed upon men to hold up Parties, or
to keep up fome Man or Parties Reputation; imaginations
which.

which men are fond of, becaufe they are their own, at leaft theirs whom they have in great Veneration or Efteem.

5. Again, the fond Miftakes of men in this kind, are obfervable in very flight and trivial matters, which yet are entertained with a kind of Religious Veneration, when they ferve to hold up Parties, or as difciminations of their Profeffions. Among the profeffed *Monks and Fryars* they have certain Habits affigned to feveral Orders, and as well anciently as now have feveral kinds of *Tonfures* of their Heads, which they obferve with great feverity ; and place much Religion in them.

And even among the various Sects, or Perfwafions among thofe that at leaft abhor Popery, yet we fhall find fome fuch *fond things* upon which they lay a great weight of their Religion : fometimes in very *Looks* and compofing of their Countenance ; fometimes in the manner or Tone of Expreffions; fometimes in *affected Phrafes*; fometimes in *Geftures*, fometimes in *Habits* and *Dreffes*, fometimes in ufe of *Meats and Drinks* of one kind or another. I fhall give fome few Inftances :

You fhall have fome that place a great point of Religion in forbearing the *eating of Flefh upon Frydays*, or in the time of *Lent*, but yet indulge themfelves oftentimes in the eating of the choiceft Fifh, and the moft coftly Diet of other Meats : Others again think they muft needs go as far on the other Extreme, Chufing thofe Seafons for Feafting upon Flefh, and think it acceptable to God, becaufe it runs counter to the other Exteme.

Again, a time there was when it was thought that *long Hair* was unbecoming Profeffors of Chriftianity, and upon that account fome did wear their *Hair* fhort, even to extremity. But about the beginning of the late Wars, many took up, as they thought, a more elevated way of Chriftianity, and as a Badg thereof wore their Hair extreme Long.

TheConformifts ufually wear Gowns or Canonical Coats;

Many

Many of the Nonconformifts by way of Difcrimination ufe other Habits.

The *former* officiate, as the Canons require them, in Surplices, and fometimes with Hoods, and fome are fo taken with it, that they think the Offices want an Effential Part when performed without it ; fome of the *latter* think the folemn Ordinances are profaned by it, and rendred Superftitious.

But among all the differing Perfwafions among us, there are none that give a man more ample Evidence of Miftakes of this Nature, than thofe called *Quakers*, who place a great part of their Religion in keeping on their Hats, in ufing the words *Thee* and *Thou*, in ftiling the Months and Days of the Week not according to the ufual Appellation, but the firft, or fecond month, or day, in certain Habits and Poftures unlike other men ; in Silent Devotions at their Publck Meetings, in *revileing* and *crying down* the Eftablifhed Miniftry, Churches, Sacraments, *Lords-day*, and all manner of Forms, whether commanded or ufed by others; in refufing to take an Oath when lawfully called thereunto ; and fome fuch other fingularities. Take away but thefe, and the like affected Superadditions, the men are as other men, fome indeed very fober, honeft, juft and plain-hearted men, and found in moft, if not all the important Doctrines and Practices of Chriftianity ; others (as it happens in all Profeffions) Subtle, Covetous, Uncharitable Tumultuous, Ignorant, proud Defpifers of others, Slanderers, and yet as long as they conform to their *Sect* in thefe impertinent or unwarrantable fingularities, they pleafe themfelves with the Stile of the *People of God*, and are for the moft part efteemed fuch by thofe of that Sect.

By this little Survey, we may eafily take an Eftimate of the Miftakes of Mankind, and even among Chriftians, touching the Miftakes in point of Chriftianity and Chriftian Religion,

Religion, and how common it is to mifplace the *Name* of Chriſtian Religion and the *Nature* of it, and attribute it to ſuch things as in truth have nothing to do with it,but many times are directly contrary to it.

And yet even in theſe Impertinencies many men place the greateſt moment of their Religion, and have as great and many times a greater zeal and fervour for them, than for the weighty Points and Duties of Chriſtianity, and moſt of the buſineſs of many men Conſiſts in Velitations and Defences and Invectives about them; The Pulpits and the Preſs is ingaged about them. Love, and Charity, and even common Humanity, and mutual Converſation between Man and Man, Church and Church, Party, and Party, is broken by the Mutual colliſions and animoſities concerning them. So that (the Lord be merciful to us and forgive us) there is as little love, and as great diſtance and animoſity between many of the Diſſenting Parties a-mong Proteſtants, touching theſe Matters, as there is between Papiſts and Proteſtants, or between Chriſtians and Infidels. And by this means the true Life of Chriſtian Religion, and that which was the great End of its Inſti-tution, and the true genuine and natural Effect of it upon the heart and foul, and courſe of life, is loſt or neglected by them that profeſs it, or diſparaged among thoſe that either have not entertained it, or at leaſt enter-tained it as they do the Cuſtoms of the Country wherein they are educated. Theſe men, when they ſee ſo much Religion placed by Profeſſors of Chriſtianity in theſe things, which every intelligent man values but as Forms, or In-ventions, or Modes, or Artifices, and yet as great weight laid upon them, as great fervour and animoſity uſed for or againſt them, as almoſt for any Points of Chriſtian Re-ligion, they are preſently apt to cenſure and throw off all Religion, and reckon all of the ſame make.

But

But when all is done, true Chriſtian Religion is a thing of another kind of Make, and is of another kind of Efficacy, and directed unto, and effective of a nobler End, than thoſe things about which, as above is ſaid, men ſo much contend, and that makes ſo great a buſtle and noiſe in the world. As the *Credenda* are but few and plain, ſo the *Facienda*, or things to be done, are ſuch as do truly ennoble and advance the Humane Nature, and brings it to its due habitude, both to God and Man.

It teacheth and tutors the ſoul to a high reverence and ve-neration of Almighty God, a ſincere and upright walking as in the preſence of the Inviſible, All-ſeeing God : It makes a man truly to love, to honour, to obey him, and therefore careful to know what his will is; it renders the heart highly thankful to him, both as his Creator, Redee-mer, and Benefactor : It makes a man entirely to depend upon, to ſeek to him for guidance, and direction, and protection ; to ſubmit to his Will with all Patience, and Reſignation of Soul : It gives the law not only to his Word and Actions, but to his very Thoughts and Purpo-ſes, that he dares not entertain a very thought unbecom-ing the ſight and preſence of that God to whom all our thoughts are legible : It teacheth and bringeth a man to ſuch a deportment both of external and internal ſobriety, as may be decent in the preſence of God and all his holy An-gels : It cruſheth and Caſts down all Pride and Haughtineſs both in a mans heart and carriage, and gives him an hum-ble frame of ſoul and life, both in the ſight of God and men : It regulates and governs the Paſſions of the Mind, and brings them into due moderation and frame : It gives a man a right eſtimate of this preſent world, and ſets the heart and hopes above it, ſo that he never loves it more than it deſerves: It makes the Wealth and Glory of this World, high Places, and great Preferments, but of a low and

D

little

little value to him ; fo that he is neither covetous nor ambitious, nor over follicitous concerning the advantages of it :
It brings a man to that frame that Righteoufnefs, Juftice,
Honefty, and Fidelity is as it were part of his Nature ; he
can fooner dye than commit or purpofe that which is unjuft,
difhoneft, or unworthy a good man: It makes him value
the love of God and peace of Confcience above all the
Wealth and Honours in the World, and be very vigilant to
keep it inviolably : Though he be under a due apprehenfion of the love of God to him, yet it keeps him humble and
watchful, and free from all prefumption, fo that he dares not
under a vain confidence of the Indulgence, and Mercy, and
Favour of God, turn afide to commit or purpofe even the
leaft injury to man, he performs all his Duties to God in
fincerity, and integrity, and Conftancy ; and while he lives
on Earth, yet his Converfation, his Hopes, his Treafure,
and the flower of his Expectation is in Heaven, and he entirely endeavours to Walk futably to fuch a Hope : In fum,
it reftores the Image of God unto the Soul in Righteoufnefs and true Holinefs.

Compofitum jus, fafque animi fanctofque receffus
mentis, & incoctum generofo pectus honefto.

Thefe, and the like to thefe, are the Ends, Defign and Effect of True Chriftian Religion, truly received and digefted
in the Soul.   And certainly any man that duly confidereth,
will find that they are of another kind of Nature and Value,
than thofe fublime Speculations, Politick Conftitutions,
Forms or not Forms, affected Singularities, upon which
many lay the weight of Religion, and for and touching
which there is fo much Contention and Animofity in the
World.   So that methinks men in this regard are like to
a Company of foolifh Boys, who when the Nut is
broken

broken, run ſcrambling after the pieces of the Shell, and in the mean while the Kernel is neglected and loſt.

Now touching the Reaſons or Cauſes of theſe Miſapprehenſions touching Religion, they are various : ſome deſerve compaſſion, and others are more or leſs excuſable, according to their ſeveral kinds : 1. Some perſons truly Conſcientious and zealous of any thing that they judge to be diſpleaſing to God, as not agreeable to his Will, and obſerving the many Corruptions, that the *Romiſh* Church have brought into the Worſhip of God, are very ſuſpicious of any thing that may look, as they think, that way ; and therefore, though they are otherwiſe men of ſound and Orthodox Principles, and of a truly righteous, ſober, and pious Life, yet perchance are tranſported ſomewhat too far in ſcrupling or oppoſing ſome Ceremonies or Forms; And poſſibly their Education and Converſation with men of ſuch Perſwaſions have confirmed them in it, ſo that they do not oppoſe out of a frowardneſs or peeviſhneſs of Mind, or out of Pride, or a Spirit of Oppoſition, but in the ſincerity and ſimplicity of their hearts, and out of a tenderneſs for the Honour of God. Theſe, though they are or may be miſtaken in their Perſwaſions, yet certainly *deſerve Compaſſion, Tenderneſs*, yea and *Love* alſo, much rather than *Severity* or *Contempt.*

2. Others again, obſerving that certain Modes and Forms, and the rigorous Obſervations of them, are the common road for *attaining Preferments* or Favours of great Perſons, upon that account exerciſe a marvellous fervour of mind for them, and a vigorous oppoſition of all that come not up to them in every punctilio, that they may thereby be taken notice of, and imployed as uſeful and fit and vigorous Aſſertors and Inſtruments for this purpoſe.

3. Many times *Gain* and *Profit* is the End and Deſign of many Practices and Poſitions appendicated to Chriſtian Religion,

ligion, as is before obferved in the *Romifh Church*; and it is eafily obfervable that Intereft, Profit, and Temporal Advantage have a ftrong byafs upon Mens Affections, and are dearer to them than the Truth of Religion, and carry men more vigoroufly in their upholding and maintenance, than Religion it felf doth: And becaufe the prefence of zeal for Religion carries a fair Plaufibility with all men, therefore thofe very things that are but *Engines* of *Gain* and *Profit* are Chriftned with the fpecious Name of Religion.

It was the making of Silver Shrines for *Diana*, the Art whereby the Artificers got their living, that made the Out-cry, *Great is Diana of the Ephefians.*

4. Again, it is very certain that mankind hath a huge *kindnefs* and *partiality* for matters of their *own Invention*, and fet a greater rate upon them, than upon other matters handed over to them by others : And hence it comes to pafs that a new Fancy or Opinion, a new Form of Worfhip, Difcipline, or Government that, any man hath invented or ftudied out, is to fuch a man ordinarily of greater value and moment than it deferves, and fhall be maintained with greater zeal, Fervour and Animofity, than Points of greater truth and moment, as if the great moment and weight of Religion and Chriftianity lay in it, which is in truth nothing elfe but the Effect of Self-love and Self-conceit.

5. Again, though by Nature Man be a fociable Creature; yet there is in moft Men a certain Itch of Pride, which makes them affect a *Difcrimination from others*, and to become a kind of *feparated Party* more refined than the reft of the fame Common Profeffion.

I do remember in the beginning of our late *Troubles*, the *only Party* that *vifibly appeared*, were *fome* that *defired fome Reformation in Church-matters* : And when that Party had obtained, under the Name of the *Presbyterian Party*, in a very

very little while there arofe a more fublime Party of men, called the Independant or Congregational men, which much defpifed the former, as not arrived to a Juft Meafure of Reformation. Shortly after that there arofe a kind of *Lay Party*, which as much undervalued the Independant, and indeed the Miniftry in general.

After that there arofe a Party difcriminating it felf from all the former, *viz.* the *Quakers.* Thefe various Parties were as fo many Subdivifions and Rectifications of what went before.

Now the Means of holding up this *Difcrimination* of *Parties* are certain *felect Opinions, Practices,* or *Modes,* which are like the *Badges* or Colours that give each Party his Denomination, Diftinction, and Difcrimination: And confequently thefe Difcriminative Badges have as great a rate fet upon them as each Sect fets upon it felf; and therefore muft be upheld under the very Notion of the life of Religion, and muft be maintained with the greateft fervour imaginable ; for otherwife the Diftinction of the Sects themfelves would faHl to the ground, and become contemptible both among themfelves and others, becaufe otherwife there would appear very little and inconfiderable reafon, upon trifling or fmall reafons, to Separate and Divide from others, and to Un-Church and Un-Chriften them that are not. Their Company or Society.

PART

PART II.

CONCERNING

RELIGION.

The life of it, and Super additions to it.

THe Truth and Spirit of Religion comes in a narrow compafs, though the Effect and Operation thereof are large and diffufive. *Solomon* comprehended it in a few words, *Fear God, and keep his Commandments, for this is the whole Duty of man* : The foul and life of Religion is the Fear of God, which is the Principle of Obedience ; but Obedience to his Commands, which is an act or exercife of that life, is various, according to the variety of the Commands of God : If I take a Kernel of an Acorn, the Principle of life lies in it : the thing it felf is but fmall, but the Vegetable Principle that lies in it takes up a lefs room than the Kernel it felf, little more than the quantity of a fmall Pins head, as is eafy to be obferved by Experiment, but the exercife of that Spark of life is large and comprehenfive in its Operation ;

tion ; it produceth a great Tree, and in that Tree the Sap, the Body, the Bark, the Limbs, the Leaves, the Fruit ; and so it is with the Principle of True Religion, the Principle it self lies in a narrow compass, but the activity and energy of it is diffusive and various.

This Principle hath not only Productions that naturally flow from it, but where it is it ferments and assimulates, and gives a kind of Tincture even to other Actions that do not in their own Nature follow from it, as the Natur*e* and Civil Actions of our lives. Under the former was our Lords Parable of a Grain of Mustard, under the latter of his Comparison of Leven, just as we see in other things of Nature. Take a little Red Wine, and drop it into a Vessel of Water, it gives a new Tincture to the Water ; or take a grain of Salt and put it into Fresh Liquor, it doth communicate it self to the next adjacent part of the Liquor, and that again to the next, until the whole be fermented : So that small and little vital Principle of the Fear of God doth gradually and yet suddenly assimilate the actions of our life flowing from another Principle. It rectifies and moderates our Affections, and Passions, and Appetites, it gives Truth to our Speech, Sobriety to our Sences, Humility to our Parts, and the like.

· Religion is best in its *Simplicity* and *Purity*, but difficult to be retained so, without Superstructions and Accessions ; And those do commonly in time *Stifle and Choke* the *Simplicity* of Religion, unless much Care and Circumspection be used : the Contemperations are so *many* and so *Cumbersom*, that Religion loseth its *Nature*, or is *strangled* by them : Just as a man that hath some Excellent Simple Cordial or Spirit, and puts in Musk in it to make it smell sweet, and Honey to make it taste pleasant, and it may be Cantharides to make it look glorious. Indeed by the Infusions he hath given it a very *fine Smell*, and *Tast*, and *Colour*, but yet he hath so *clogg'd* it, and *sophisticated* it with Superadditions,

additions, that it may be he hath altered the Nature, and deftroyed the Virtue of it.

The Superadditions and Superftructions in Point of Religion are very, *many*, and from very many and various tempers in men that add them. As for Inftance,

1. There is one common Superaddition that naturally all men are apt to bring into it, *viz*. that it may *Gratifie the Senfe* ; for in as much as the moft powerful and immediate influence upon us comes from   and through our Senfes, and that fpiritual and internal apprehenfions have not fo ftrong or conftant an Impreffion upon us, they feem things at a diftance, flat, and the Soul is weary of bearing it felf upon them ; men are apt to drefs up Religion fo as it may be gratetul to the *Senfe* : *Make us Gods that may go before us* : And this is the *chief original* of *Idolatry*, and alfo of *Superftition*.

2. There are other Superadditions that come even from the accidental Inclinations of men to fome fpecial matter which they value and love ; and that they carry over into Religion ; and many times mingle with it. As for the purpofe, take a man greatly admiring *natural Philofophy*, he will be apt to mingle and qualifie Religion with *Philofophical Notions*. Many of thofe things of *Ariftotle* that are harfhly and difhonourably afferted concerning the Diety are from his tenacious adhering to certain Philofophical Pofitions that he had fixed upon.

Behmen, who was a great Chymift, refolves almoft all Religion in Chymiftry, and frames his Conceptions of Religion fuitable and conformable to Chymical Notions.

Socinus and his Followers, being great Mafters of Reafon, and deeply learned in matters of *Morality*, mingle almoft all Religion with it, and form Religion purely to the Model and Platform of it.

E   Many

Many great *Phificians* that have much obferved the Conftitutions of Mans Body, have figured to themfelves Notions of the Soul conformable to the Refults of their Obfervations in the Body.

And as thus in thefe forts of men, fo again men of *Me-
taphyfical* and *Notional Brains* and Education, as the Schoolmen, they have conformed Religion and their Notions
concerning it to *Metaphyficks* : and indeed have made that
which is and ought to be the common Principle for the
actuating of all men, yea even of the meaneft Capacities, to
be a meer Collection of Subtilties, far more abftrufe than
the moft intricate and fublimated Humane Learning what-
foever.

Again, take a *Polititian*, or *States-man*, and he fhall moft
eafily conform Religion to *State Policy*, and make it indeed a moft excellent and incomparable Engine for it, and
nothing elfe.

And if we narrowly look upon the Method and Syftem
of Religion as it is formed by the *Romifh Hierarchy*, it is
a moft exquifite piece of *Humane Policy*, and every thing
therein fuited with moft exquifite Art and Prudence for the
fupport of the Grandure and Intereft of that State : This
hath mingled with the Chriftian Religion the *Popes Infallibility* and *Supremacy*, his Power of *Pardoning* and *Dif-
penfing*, his *Keys of Heaven* and *Hell*, his *Purgatory* and *Indulgences*, and *Images*, and *Adorations* of them, his *Reliques*, and *Pilgrimages*, and *canonizing* of *Saints*, and a thoufand fuch kind of ftuff moft incomparably fitted to mens
Paffions and Affections; and fo to fupport that moft artificial
and methodical Fabrick of the Popifh State : for indeed it
is no other.

And if we look into other Kingdoms and Places, we fhall
eafily find that Religion is fo ftated and ordered as may beft
conduce to the peace, order, wealth, and amplitude of
                                                          every

every Kingdom; for wife Politicians, finding that Religion hath a great impreffion on mens minds, and therefore if it be not managed by the Policy of ftate, may prove an unruly Bufinefs, if it be contemperated with Mixture prejudicial to the State, and that it may be a moft excellent Engine if it can be managed and actuated for the Benefit of the ftate, do add to it much of their own, that it may be managed upon occafion, and they drefs up Religion with *State Policy*, whereby in truth it becomes nothing elfe but a meer *piece of Humane Policy*, under the Name of Religion.

And on the other fide, thofe either *politick* or *difcontented* Spirits, that would put a Kingdom into Blood and Confufion, do mingle *Difcontents*, and *Fancies*, and *Imaginations*, *Sufpicions* and *Frowardnefs* with Religion, and call this confufed mixture of Phancies and Paffions, *Religion*: and manage and brandifh this Weapon with mighty difadvantage to that State which they oppofe.

For it is moft apparent, that as nothing hath fo great an impulfion upon men, as that which comes under the apprehenfion of *Religion*, in as much as it concerns the greateft good, even their Everlafting Souls and Happinefs; fo nothing is of fo univerfal Concernment as this, and therefore like to attract the moft Followers; for every man hath not an *Eftate* to care for; but every man hath a *Soul* to care for; and hence it is that fcarce any great Conteft between Princes hath happened in thefe latter years, nor fcarce any Commotion in a State, but *Religion* is owned on *all fides*; and *God*, and *his Caufe*, and his *Church*, owned on on *all hands*, and therefore ftill the fcramble is for *Religion*, and who fhall keep the *Opinion of Religion* moft firm to them, and therefore they *on all hands* infufe into the thing they call *Religion* thofe things that may moft probably and politickly hold to their Party.

Again, in Conteft among *Clergymen*, every one Trims and

Orders Religion in that Dreſs that may moſt make it *their own*, and ſecure it to *themſelves.*

Take the *Popiſh Clergiemen* : hold what you will, if you hold not the *Supremacy* and *Vicariot* of the Pope, all the reſt of your Religion is not worth a ruſh.

Come to the *Reformed Epiſcopal Clergy*: **as to** the *Popes Supremacy* they diſclaim it : but if you acknowledge not *Epiſcopal Government* ; if you *ſwear not Canonical Obedience* to your *Ordinary,*if you ſubmit not to the *Liturgie,*and *Ceremonies*, and *Veſtments*, and *Muſick* uſed in the Church, you are at beſt a *Schiſmatick.*

Again, come to the *Presbyterian Clergy*, they will tell you Epiſcopal Government is *Romiſh* and *Superſtitious,* and their *Ceremonies* and Uſages Antichriſtian Uſurpations; but if you mean to be of a warrantable Religion, you muſt ſubmit to the *Presbyterian* Government as truly Apoſtolical.

Come to the *Independent,*he declaims againſt both the former, and tells you that the true Conformity to Apoſtolical Order is in the Congregational way.

Take the *Anabaptiſt*, and he tells you all the former are vain and irreligious, unleſs you will be *rebaptized* and *liſted* in their Church.

Again, in Points of *Doctrine*, as well as Diſcipline, it is moſt plain that Tenents are profeſſed or decryed for *diſtinction of Parties*: witneſs the Conteſt between the *Arminian* Party and the *Calviniſtical* Party, which are only uſed as Methods on either ſide, to attract Proſelytes, and diſtinguiſh Parties: And in theſe and the like diſtinctions of Parties and Profeſſions the Superſtructions and Additions are in a manner incorporated and grafted into Religion, and in effect give the only Denomination to it, according to the various Intereſts and Affections of Parties ; when in truth, the main buſineſs of theſe and the like Additions and Superſtructions,

Superſtructions, are but Policies to diſtinguiſh, and fortifie, and increaſe Parties.

3. The re are ſome *Superadditions* to Religion, that though I do not think they are to be *condemned*, yet are carefully to be *diſtinguiſhed* from the true and natural *Life of Religion*; and ſo long as they are kept under that apprehenſion, they may, if *prudently applyed* and *managed*, do good. But if either they are *imprudently inſtituted*, *imprudently applyed*, or *inconſiderately over-valued*, as if they were *Religion*, they may and many times do harm; and ſuch are decent and inoffenſive Forms in the External Worſhip of God appointed by the Civil Magiſtrate, by the advice of thoſe that are deſervedly eminent in the Church for their Piety, Learning, and Prudence. And there ſeems to be very good Reaſon for it.

1. Becauſe if every man ſhould be left to himſelf, there would Confuſion enſue ; becauſe no man knew anothers Mind, or Rule of his external Deportment.

2. All men have not that equal Prudence to Judge what were fit to be uſed: the Magiſtrate is like to make choice of thoſe perſons that are fitteſt to adviſe, and their Recommendations would be of greateſt authority with others.

3. It is moſt certain, that Man being compoſed of Soul and Body, cannot ſo regularly and well fix himſelf to his Duty, without ſome juſtifiable help to his Devotion; ſuch are vocal Prayers, Kneeling, and other Geſtures proper for the Matter of Worſhip which he intends.

And this may be one Reaſon, why the Lord, though he ſtrictly forbad all Idolatry and Superſtition, and Heatheniſh Practice to the *Jews*, yet did appoint Sacrifices, Prieſts, a glorious Tabernacle, and the Ark, which was not only a diverſion from the *Egyptian* Idolatry which they had ſeen, but alſo a help to their natural infirmity for the excitation of their Devotion.

And

And although our Lord Jefus came to *abrogate* even that *Indulgence*, and foretold that thofe *that worfhipped the Father, fhould worfhip him in Spirit and in Truth*, under the Gofpel, yet it is certain that the immediate Apoftles of Chrift did fet certain orderly Obfervances in the Church for decencies fake : and it was juftly allowable : As concerning the order of the exercife of their Supernatural Gifts, Concerning Womens fpeaking in the Church, concerning mens being covered in the Church, and Women vailed, concerning the manner and order of receiving the Sacrament, and the like.

But as there be Reafons for it, fo there be Cautions to be ufed in it.

1. That they be not too *numerous* ; for their Multitude will rather opprefs than fecure Religion.

2. That in their Natures they be not *Superftitious*, but keep as much diftance from it as well may be; otherwife they will be in Religion, as the dead Fly in the Apothecaries Oyntment.

3. That they be clean and decent, not too full of *Pomp* or *Oftentation* : Ceremonies fhould be ufed as we ufe a Glafs, rather to *preferve* the Oyl, than to *adorn* it. Too much Pomp caufeth Jealoufies even in *good men*, of a degeneration either to Jewifh Ceremonies or Popifh Vanities.

4. That though fuch are not to be *rejected* becaufe they are *Ancient*, fo if they become *Unfeafonable*, they are not to be *held* meerly becaufe they are *Ancient*. It is with Ceremonies as with fome other things that are fit to be changed when they become unufeful or offenfive, as the *Love-Feafts, Extreme Unction*, and fome other things, poffibly practifed, and fit enough, in the Primitive times : Many Ceremonies were at firft invented and practifed, to win over unconverted Heathens ; to incourage weak Chriftians, efpecially the *Jews*, who were not eafily to be drawn from
their

their Legal Ceremonies: But when People become a Knowing People, that fee beyond thofe Ceremonies, and under-
ftand when, and why, and how they came in, then it were
Prudence to *difpenfe* with, or *change* them.

5. That they *be not urged with too much rigour* or *feverity*
upon fuch as *confcientioufly* refufe them.　Charity to a weak
Brother in things indifferent in their own Nature, is then to
be exercifed, when my Brother is offended therewith, or
never: And if it be faid it is his duty to fubmit to the
Church, and not the Church to him ; I do think that anfwer
will not ferve in this cafe ; for furely though a Child owes
a Duty to a Father, yet his neglect thereof, efpecially if
it be upon a confcientious account, will not excufe the neglect of a Fathers Duty to his Child: The Apoftle profeffed
he would abftain from things lawful rather than offend his
weak Brother.

6. And efpecially that we be careful to remember, that
Religion is another thing from thefe Ceremonies.　Thefe are
of *ufe, i. e.* for *Ornament* ; They are the *Dreffings* and the
Trimmings of Religion at the beft, but the Fear of God is of
a higher extraction.

It is a pitiful thing to fee men run upon this miftake, efpecially in thefe latter times ; one placing all his Religion
in holding the *Pope to be Chrifts Vicar*, another placing Religion in this, to hold *no* Papift *can be faved* : One holding all
Religion to confift, in holding *Epifcopacy* to be *jure divino* ;
another by holding *Presbytery* to be *jure divino* ; another in
crying up *Congregational* Government ; another in *Anabap-
tife* ; one in placing all Religion in the ftrict obfervation of
all *Ceremonies* ; another in a ftrict *refufal* of all : One holding a great part of Religion in putting *off the Hat,* and
bowing at the *Name of Jefus* ; another judging a man an Ido-
later for it: and a third placing his Religion in putting off
his Hat to none ; and fo like a company of Boys that blow

Bubbles

Bubbles out of a Wall-nut-shell, every one runs after his bubble, and calls it *Religion*; and every one measures the Religion or irreligion of another, by their agreeing or dissenting with them in these or the like matters; and at best, while we scramble and wrangle about the pieces of the Shell, the Kernel is either lost, or gotten by some that doth not prize any of their Contests.

☞ Believe it, Religion is quite another thing from all these Matters: He that fears the Lord of Heaven and Earth, walks humbly before him, thankfully lays hold of the Message of Redemption by Christ Jesus, strives to express his thankfulness by the Sincerity of his Obedience, is sorry with all his soul when he comes short of his Duty, walks watchfully in the denial of himself, and holds no confederacy with any Lust or known Sin, if he falls in the least measure is restless till he hath made his Peace by true Repentance, is true in his Promise, just in his Actions; Charitable to the Poor, sincere in his Devotions, that will not deliberately dishonour God, though with the greatest security of impunity; that hath his hope in Heaven, and his Conversation in Heaven, that dare not do an Unjust Act though never so much to his advantage, and all this because he sees him that is invisible, and fears him because he loves him, fears him as well for his Goodness as his Greatness; such a man, whether he be an *Episcopal*, or a *Presbyterian*, or an *Independant*, or an *Anabaptist*; whether he wears a *Surplice*, or wears none, whether he *hears Organs*, or *hears none*, whether he Kneels at the *Communion*, or for Conscience sake *stands* or sits; he hath the *Life of Religion* in him, and that life acts in him, and will conform his soul to the Image of his Saviour, and walk along with him to Eternity, notwithstanding his *Practise* or *Non-practise* of these *Indifferents*.

☞ On the other side, if a man *fears not the Eternal* God, dares

dares commit any fin with prefumption, can drink excef-
fively, fwear vainly or falfly, commit Adultery, Lye, Co-
zen, Cheat, break his Promifes, live loofely, though he pra-
ctife every Ceremony never fo curioufly, or as ftubbornly
oppofe them; though he cry down Bifhops, or cry down
Presbytery; though he be re-baptized every day, or though
he difclaim againft it as Herefie; though he Faft all the
Lent, or Feafts out of pretence of avoiding Superftition, yet
notwithftanding thefe, and a thoufand more external Con-
formities, or zealous Oppofitions of them, he wants the
Life of Religion.

F   PART

.

PART III.

OF THE
CHRISTIAN RELIGION.

The Superstructions upon it, and Animosities about them.

THe Christian Religion and Doctrine was by the Goodnefs and Wifdom of God defigned to be the common Means and Method to bring Mankind to their Chief End, namely, to know, and to ferve, and obey, and glorifie, and everlaftingly to enjoy Almighty God the Chiefeft Good.

And to that end it was given out with all the Plainnefs and Perfpicuity, with all Evidence and certainty ; a Doctrine and Religion containing Precepts of all Holinefs and Purity, of all Righteoufnefs and Honefty, of all Longanimity, Benignity, and Gentlenefs, Sweetnefs, Meeknefs, and Charity; of all Moderation and Patience, of all Sobriety and Temperance ; in brief, it is a Religion that is admirably and fufficiently conftituted to make a man, what indeed he fhould be, Pious towards God, Juft and Beneficent towards Men, and temperate in himfelf, fitted for a life of Piety,

Honefty,

Honefty, Juftice, and Goodnefs, and Happinefs heareafter. Such is the Chriftian Religion, and fuch the men muft be that are truly conformable to it; and if any man profeffing Chriftianity, be not fuch a man, it is because he comes fo much fhort of his due Conformity to Chriftian Religion, and the moft excellent Doctrine and Precepts thereof.

The Profeffion of this Religion is that which is, and for many Ages hath been, commonly made by a very confiderable part of the known World, as the only true Religion given to the world by Almighty God, through his Son Jefus Chrift, wherein and whereby they may expect everlafting Salvation. —

But yet together with this Chriftian Religion, the Profeffors thereof have in feveral Ages and Places chofen to themfelves various *adventitious accidental Superftructions. Additions, Opinions, Modes,* and *Practices,* which they have as it were incorporated into the Chriftian Religion by them profeffed, or appendicated unto it

And thefe Superftructions or Appendixes of Chriftian Religion have been introduced and entertained by various Means, and by various Defigns, and to various Ends: Some by the *Authority of great Names* ; Some by *infenfible graditions* or long *cuftoms*, fome by a *fuppofed congruity* or *incongruity* ; fome for *Order* or *Decency:* Some for *Difcrimination* of *Parties;* Some for *Political Ends,* appearing in themfelves, or fecretly carryed on ; fome upon *emergent occafions* ; either continuing or now ceafing ; Some by Civil, fome by *Ecclefiaftical Sanctions;* Some by *traditional* Obfervations, either continued, or interrupted and revived; Some for *Ornament* ; Some for *Ufe* ; Some as fuppofed neceffary *confequents* upon the Chriftian Doctrine, Some to be, *quafi fepta & munimenta doctrinæ & religionis Evangelicæ,* as the Jewifh Traditions were fuppofed to be the *Sepimenta Legis* ; Some for one end, and fome for another :
And

And although thefe are not truly and effentially parts of the Chriftian Religion, yet as the humours in the body are fome good, fome noxious, fome innocent, though they are no part of the true vital blood, yet they mingle with it, and run along in it ; fo thefe Superftructions, and Occafions, and Additions have in various Ages, Succeffions, and Places mingled with the true radical vital Doctrine and Religion of Chrift, in mens Opinions, and Practices, and Profeffions.

And yet it is vifible to any man that will but attentively obferve the Courfes of men profeffing Chriftian Religion, that the greateft fervour and animofity of the Profeffors of Chriftian Religion is not fo much with refpect to the fubftantials of Chriftian Religion, either in things to be believed or practifed, as touching thefe *Additions* and *Superftructions* ; fome as fervently contending for them, as if the life of Chriftianity confifted in them, fome as bitterly and feverely contefting againft them, as if the life and foul of Chriftian Religion were not poffibly confifting with them.

And by thefe means thefe unhappy Confequences follow.

1. That whereas the main of Chriftian Religion confifts in the true belief of the Gofpel of Chrift Jefus, and the Practice of thofe Chriftian Virtues that he left unto his Difciples and Followers, both by his Example and Precept, namely love of God, Holinefs and Purity of life, Humility and Lowlinefs of mind, Patience, Meeknefs, Gentlenefs, Charity, a low and eafy Value of the World, Contentation of Mind, fubmiffion to the Will of God, Dependance upon him, Refignation unto him, and other excellent Evangelical Virtues, that perfect and rectifie the Soul, and fit it for an humble Communion with Almighty God in this life, and a bleffed fruition of his Prefence in the life to come; the Chriftian Religion is not fo much placed in thefe, as in an entire *Conformity to Modes and Circumftances*, or an extream Averfion

fion from them. And according to the various Interests or Inclinations of Parties those are made the *Magnalia* of Christian Religion, and such as give the only Character or Discriminative Indication of the Christian Religion.

2. And consequently all the greatest part of that stress and *fervour of mind*, which should be employed in those great weighty Substantials of Christianity, runs out and spends it self in those little Collaterals, and Superstructions, and Additaments, some placing the greatest earnestness and intention, contention of mind to have them, and some placing the intension and fervour of their mind to be without them, not unlike those old Contentions between the *Eastern* and *Western* Churches touching the time of the Paschal Observation, one Party excommunicating the other for their dissent, as if the whole weight and stress of the Christian Religion lay in those little Additaments.

3. And hereupon there arise Schismes, Factions, and personal Animosities, Discrimination of Parties, Censorioufness, and studied estrangings of Professors of Christianity, oftentimes one Party declining those Practices which are good and commendable in the other, to keep their distances the more irreconcilable, and each Party espousing some odd Discriminating Habits, Modes; and sometimes also by Opinions in matters of Religion, that may estrange and discriminate them each from the other; and these Opinions though of little moment or consequence (it may be whether true or false) are advanced up into little less than Articles of Faith, for the sake of this Discrimination, when possibly they are of little moment whether they be assented unto or not, of less certainty, and have little or no influence or concern in the Substance of Christian Doctrine.

4. And hereupon it oftentimes comes to pass that not only the common Bond of Charity and Christian Love is broken between the Professors of the same substantials in Christianity,

Chriſtianity, but there is moſt ordinarily much more *Severity*, and *Perſecution*, and *Implacableneſs*, and *Irreconcileableneſs*, more endeavours to undermine, and ſupplant, and diſgrace Diſſenters, more ſcorns, and vilifying, and reproach, and inſolence one towards another in their viciſſitudes of advantage, than there is between Profeſſors of Chriſtianity, and men of the moſt looſe and profane lives, between Orthodox and Heretiques, nay between Chriſtians and Turks, or Infidels many times.

5. And from this there ariſeth a moſt fruitful and a moſt inevitable increaſe of Atheiſm and contempt of Religion, in many of the Spectators of this Game among Profeſſors of the Chriſtian Religion, and that upon theſe two Accounts: Principally, becauſe when they hear each Party declare (as they muſt if they declare truth) in their Sermons and Writings, that the Doctrine of Chriſtianity injoynes *Mutual Love*, Condeſcention, Charity, Gentleneſs, Meekneſs, and yet ſo little practiſed by Diſſenting Parties, men are apt to conclude, that either theſe perſons do not believe what they pretend to preach and publiſh, or that the Doctrine of Chriſtianity was a Notion and Speculation, and never intended as a neceſſary Rule of Practice, ſince the greateſt Pretenders to the Religion of Chriſt practiſe ſo little of it.

2. Becauſe when men ſee that thoſe little Superſtructions and Additions are by the one ſide *proſecuted*, and on the other ſide *decryed*, with as much animoſity, fervour and ſeverities, as the moſt weighty and important Truths and Precepts of Evangelical Faith and Obedience, Spectators and By-ſtanders think that they are all of the ſame value; and when they ſee that theſe things which every ſober conſiderate man muſt needs conclude little, and of no momont, are rated at ſo great a value by the conteſting Parties of each ſide, Truths then are doubted of in relation to theſe : It makes men call in queſtion great matters, when they ſee ſuch ſmall things purſued or declined with no leſs Fervour and Animoſity than if they were of the greateſt.   And

And confidering thefe unhappy Confequences of thefe fervours of minds touching thefe fmall Appendixes and Superftructions, even more than about, or concerning the very weighty things of the Gofpel, I have endeavoured to fearch out the Reafon how this ftrong Diftemper comes to pafs ; and there feems to be thefe Caufes thereof.

1. Ordinarily a man is more fond of, and concerned for fomething that *is his own*, than for that which is *of God* ; as we are tranfported with a Love to our*felves*, fo we are tranfported with a love and admiration of what is *our own* : and hence it is that the weightier and more important Duties injoined by Chrift, partake lefs of our zeal, or courage, or intenfion of mind, than our *own little Fantafies* and *Inventions.*

2. *Pride, Credit, and Reputation* are commonly ingaged in either Party in the things contefted, when they are once contefted ; and thefe are violent and preffing Interefts and Motions.

3. The *Plaineft Truth* and *Purity* of Religion is a thing that feldom *pleafeth and futeth to the* Curiofity and Appetite of Men; they are always fond of fomething Annexed or Appendicated to Religion to make it pleafing to their Appetite. A certain Sawce that may entertain their Fancy, after which it may run, and wherein it may pleafe it felf. And thefe Sawces to Religion are various, and varioufly pleafing, according to the Various Inclinations of Men : Moft ordinarily the Fancies of men affect fome things Splendid and Senfible to be Superadded to Religion ; the *Ifraelites* would needs have gods that might go before them ; and in complyance with this Humour, moft of the Strange Modes and Gefticulations among the Heathens, and moft of the Superftitions, Ceremonies and Rites among the Papifts were invented.

Again, fometimes the Humour of the People runs in the
other

other Extreme, either they will have nothing of Form or Order, or all such Forms or Orders as are extremely oppo-site to what others use, and place their delight and com-placency therein: And by this means oftentimes it comes to pass, that men are carried with greater earnestness and ve-hemence after those *Placentia,* the entertainments of their fancies, than to the true Substance of Religion it self.

4. Oftentimes it comes to pass that there are two very *jealous Concerns,* and impatient of any Corrival, that are ingaged each against other in these different and dissenting Practices, relating to Collaterals in Religion: On the one side, *Power and Authority* is very tender of its own Interest, and jealous of a Competitor or Rival: On the other side, *Conscience* and *Perswasion* either of the *Necessity* or *Unlawfulness* of any thing, is very jealous, or fearful, and suspicious of any thing that might injure it : And whether the Consci-ence be mistaken or not, yet so long as its Perswasion, that is entertained *sub ratione conscientiæ,* prevails, this jealousie will still prevail in the mind ; and it many times falls out that *Authority* on the one hand is impatient, or at least jea-lous of Opposition, and *Conscience* on the other hand restless and unquiet.

5. And the difficulty is so much the greater, because each seems to derive their obliging Authority from God ; the Magistrate recognizing God Almighty as the Fountain, Root, and Foundation of his Power; and the Conscience supposed to be the Vicegerent of God in the Soul.

6. But that which admirably keeps up these differences, is that men on each side, deal not one with another *calmly,* *mildly,* or upon the Reasons of the things, or upon a true way of Reasoning, Debating, and Arguing of things, or prudent Considerations that might invite yielding on the one side, or accommodations of the other, but each Party takes in all those Contributions, Assistances, and Advantages, that

G   common-

commonly accompany the worſt of Contentions.

For inſtance, 1. Extremity of Paſſion and Indignation, 2. Violence and Bitterneſs of Writings and Speeches, 3. Each Party rendring the other as odious and ridiculous as is poſſible : 4. Scoffing, jearing, and perſonal reflections : 5. Artifices and Deſigns each to catch and undermine the other: 6. An induſtrious and willing miſ-interpretation of each others Words, Writings, and Actions, and raiſing them to odious Inferences and Conſequences, beyond what they were meant, or really and truly bear. 7. Diſingenuous Quotations out of each other, without thoſe ordinary Remedies that might be allowed by comparing of other parts of their Writings.

Theſe and the like Auxiliaries are on each part taken into theſe Velitations between Chriſtians, and in relation to things contended for or againſt in theſe Differences, whereas the whole tenour of the Doctrine of Chriſtianity, as it was delivered by Chriſt and his Apoſtles, decries nothing more than Anger, Wrath, Malice, Railing, Evil-ſpeaking, Backbiting Slanders, Reproches, Names and Epithets of Scorns, Craft, and Subtilty ; yet all theſe black Legions are called, uſed, and imployed in the management of that Cauſe, which each Party pretends to be the Cauſe of Chriſt ; as if Fiends, and Furies, and Legions of Devils were thought fit Auxiliaries on each Party, wherein both pretend the intereſt of Chriſt Jeſus.

And that this is ſo, let any man but read thoſe Books which have flown abroad from either Party, he will find it evident in all the Contentions of this nature : Witneſs on the one part *Martin Marprelate*, the *Odious Centuries* put out by Mr. *White* in the beginning of the Long Parliament, the frequent Invectives and odious Epithets given to Liturgy, to the Biſhops, Conforming Miniſters, and to the Church of *England* it ſelf, as Antichriſtian, Idolatrous, *Babyloniſh,*

Babylonish, and a thousand such Names and Stiles.

And on the other side there have been many that have not been behind hand with bitter Invectives, Scornful and mocking Expressions and Appellations, odious Reflections, unnecessary to be repeated. By all which these two things are evident,

1. That these Transports of either side come not from that Spirit which Christ brought with him into the world, and which he commended and left to his Disciples and Followers; namely, a Spirit of Love, of Charity, of Gentleness, Patience, Kindness, and Sweetness of disposition.

2. That if men go about to justifie this, because first provoked by the adverse Party, and so justifie it by the Law of Taliation, these men do not remember that as on the one hand the Duty of Christians is Self-denial, Moderation, and Peaceableness; on the other side, that a Spirit of Revenge, an Eye for an Eye, a Tooth for a Tooth, is as much against the Doctrine of Christ, as any thing in the world.

Therefore certainly it becomes those of either Party either to cashier these black Auxiliaries of their Wars, and Contentions of this kind, or otherwise for the sake and honour of Christ and the Christian Religion, plainly declare that he is not concerned in the Contest, but that the Contest is a Contest of *Interest* and *Vain-Glory*, of *Pride* and *Ambition*, and *Reputation*, and *desire of Victory*; Or if they will not declare so much to the World, yet they must give leave to the Spectators to judge of it so.

Now these bitternesses and virulentnesses of either side, have been commonly of two kinds: first, such as reflect, if not all together, yet most of all, upon the *Persons* of their Adversaries. 2. Or such as reflect only upon the *Matters* in difference between them; both were bad enough, and such as serve to make the Differences and Breaches wider.

But of late times, I know not by what unhappy Star,

there

there hath prevailed more than formerly, certain Invectives that have gone much farther, even to the rendring of
Religion it self, and *Scripture Expreſſions* ridiculous, and pieces of raillery ; and I could have wiſhed that ſome late
Books, put out under the faſhion of *Dialogues,* and ſome
other Books of that kind, had not been too Guilty of this
fault.

I do remember when *Ben. Johnſon* made his Play of the
Alchymiſt, wherein he brings in *Anartas* in deriſion of
the perſons then called *Puritans,* with many of their Phraſes in uſe among them, taken out of the Scriptures ;
with a deſign to render that ſort of perſons ridiculous,
and to gain applauſe to his wit and fancy. But although
thoſe perſons were not in very good eſteem among the
Great Ones and Gallants, yet the Play was diſliked, and
indeed abhorred, becauſe it ſeemed to reproach Religion
it ſelf, though intended only to render the Puritans ridiculous. That which was uncomely and unſeemly in a
Poet, who made it his buſineſs to make Plays, certainly
is much more fulſom and unſavoury in another; eſpecially if the Author be a *Clergy-man,* as I ſuppoſe he is :
for of all men in the world it becomes ſuch *proſpicere heno-
ri Religionis Chriſtianæ,* and not to render it ridiculous
and contemptible, by raillery and ſcurrilous jeaſting.

And yet I do not find in all *Ben. Johnſon's Alchymiſt* one
half of thoſe ridiculous and unſeemly repetitions of Scripture Phraſes and Expreſſions, as well as mimical imitations
and diſdainful mockings of thoſe Perſons, and that Party
whom he deſigns to diſparage : Scarce a Page but ſome un-
handſom mention of the *Spirit,* and *Chriſt* and *Grace,* and
Saints, and ſome Scripture Expreſſions : And if it ſhall be
ſaid that he doth it but only in exprobration of ſuch perſons
as abuſed or miſapplyed ſuch expreſſions, and it is not
with intent to reproach the Scripture or thoſe Phraſes that
are

are defumed from it, but to fhew the boldnefs and miftakes of them that have mifapplied or abufed them.

I anfwer, That thefe Mifapplications and inconfiderate Ufes of Scripture-phrafes by them, though it be juftly reprovable, yet it is far more intollerable in him. Though their miftakes were weak and foolifh, yet they were *ferious* in thofe very miftakes ; but this man induftrioufly and defignedly makes the *Expreffion ridiculous* and contemptible. 2. Their Abufes of Scriptures and Scripture-phrafes will not at all juftifie the like in him, though in another kind, and to another end ; he might have learned to have avoided the folly and inconfiderateneſs of the others, and not have multitiplied it in himfelf by a worfe Method of abufe.

Certainly, who ever he was that made thefe *Conferences*, I dare fay he hath no fuch pattern of writing from the Apoftles or Fathers. The neareft Copy that I know of it, is the *A*——and though he feems a man of Wit and Learning, and poffibly would be fome body in the world, I dare fay they that cherifh him in the main of his defign are afhamed of his fcurrility, and wifh it had been fpared, and fo perchance may he be when more years have better confideration. The mifchiefs that come by this manner of writing are very great and many.

1. It makes Differences irreconcilable. When Differences Civil or Ecclefiaftical in Judgment or Practice happen, gentlenefs, foftnefs, mildnefs, and perfonal refpectfulnefs quiet the Paffions and Spirits of the adverfe Party, gain upon him, get within him ; and when the perfon is thus won, and over-matched with Sweetnefs and Kindnefs, and perfonal Jealoufies and Prejudices removed, Perfwafions and Arguments grow prevalent, come with their full weight, are entertained calmly, and confiderately, and infenfibly gain grounds even upon the judgment: But I yet
never

knew any man converted by an angry, paſſionate, railing Adverſary, for ſuch kind of behaviour preſently rai-
ſeth in the Adverſary the like Paſſions and Prejudice, and
makes the Diſtance greater ; and the Paſſions being ingaged in the quarrel, the Judgments of both ſides are loſt,or
blinded, or ſilenced with the duſt and noiſe of paſſionate
digladiations ; and indeed conſidering how apparently and
evidently ſuch kind of dealing between Diſſenters renders
compoſures almoſt impoſſible ; and yet obſerving how
much this courſe of reviling, and opprobrious, and unman-
ly as well as unchriſtian Language, is in practiſe, I
thought that it hath been a real deſign to render each Party odious and irreconcilable to the other, and the hopes
of compoſure deſperate : For who can ever expect that any
man, or any ſort of men, ſhould be drawn over to that
Party that ſhall publickly ſtile him *brain-ſick*, a *fool, ſilly,
hypocrite, fanatique*, and a hundred ſuch ſcornful Appellations; or that men will be eaſily drawn to relinquiſh thoſe
Opinions or Perſwaſions when they muſt thereby in effect
ſubſcribe to ſuch Epithetes and Appellations before all the
world ; and of all things in the world men can with the
leaſt patience bear reflection upon their intellectuals, and
are moſt irreconcilable to them that traduce or abuſe them
therein.

2. It greatly diſadvantageth the *Cauſe*, as well as the
Perſons of thoſe that uſe this method amongſt ſober indifferent Obſervers, who will be ready to conclude them
a parcel of people tranſported by paſſions, weak, and pre-
judicated ; and look upon ſuch a Cauſe as is maintained by
railing, ſcoffing, raillery, and unproved Calumnies, as
weak, and ſtanding in need of ſuch rudeneſſes to ſupport
and maintain it.

3. It expoſeth Religion it ſelf to the deriſion of Atheiſts,
and confirms them in their Atheiſms, and gains them too
many

many Profelytes; and that principally upon thefe Rea
fons, .1. Becaufe they find that Clergy-men do tell them
in the Pulpits, that Chrift himfelf and his Appoftles condemned railing, fcandalous Appellation, as *Raca*, and
Fool, Evil-fpeaking, foolifh-jeafting, Mocking, Reviling; This
they tell men, and they tell them truly, and yet thefe
very men that call themfelves Minifters of Chrift, Mef-
fengers of the Gofpel of Peace, take that admirable liberty of reproaching, fcoffing, and deriding one another
in their publick Pamphlets and Difcourfes, that can
fcarce be exampled among the moft invective Ranks
of Perfons, whofe trade it is to be Satyrical, and render people ridiculous : Nay fo far hath this Excellent
manage prevail'd among Clergy-men, that their Scoffs
and Reproaches are not levelled at the Perfons, or Perfonal Defects of Diffenters, but rather than want fup-
ports for their Party, will have ugly flings at Religion
it felf, at Scripture-expreffions ; and when men fee fuch
a courfe of Practice among the Preachers and Clergy-men,
they are ready to conclude, that furely they believe not
themfelves what they preach to others ; therefore think
they have a fair pretence not to believe them.

2. But principally thefe great Animofities and Tranfports
of diffenting Clergy-men, confirms and promotes A-
theifme, upon this account, that the things about which
this wonderful hate is ftrucken between thefe Parties,
are fuch as both Parties agree to be none of the Fundamentals of the Religion profeffed by both, but Ac-
ceffaries and Acceffions, and fuch indeed as By-ftanders
think are of very fmall moment, and yet when men fee fo
much heat and paffion, fo much fervour and contention,
fuch reproaches and revilings, fuch *exafperations* of
Authority on either Party, fuch mutual Profecutions one
of another, that more could not poffibly be done between

tween Diffenters in thofe points which both agree to
be Fundamental, Atheiftical fpirits are apt to conclude,
that probably thofe points, that both fides fuppofed to
be of greater moment, are *ejufdem farinæ*, with thofe
in Conteft, fince they are not, nor cannot be profecuted
with greater fervour, than thefe which all men take to
be fmall and inconfiderable, and that it is Intereft, Vain-
glory, and Applaufe, or fome other Temporal Concern,
that gives this Fervour and Zeal in Matters of Religion,
more than the true Concerns of it felf. The Conclufion
therefore is, That men for their own fakes, and for the
fake and honour of the Chriftian Religion, would ufe
more Temperance, Prudence, and Moderation, in Con-
tefts about Circumftantials.

Sir

Sir. Francis Bacon Lord Verulam, *Viscount St.* Albans *and Lord Chancellor after, in his Advertisement of the Controversies, of the Church of* England, pag. 138. *of his Works.*

THe wrongs of them who are possessed of the Government of the Church, towards the other, may hardly be dissembled, or excused: They have charged them as tho' they denyed tribute to *Cæsar*, and withdrew from the Civil Magistrate, the obedience which they have ever performed and taught.

I have oft transcribed Bishop Andrews *Confident Assertion of the Loyalty of those then called Puritans, against the Papists accusation, in his* Tortura Torti.

They have sorted and coupled them with the Family of Love, whose Heresie they have labour'd to destroy and confute. They have been swift of Credit to receive accusations against them, from those that have quarrelled with them, but for speaking against sin and Vice. Their Accusations and Inquisitions have been strict, Swearing men to *Blanks* and *Generalities*, not included within compass of Matter certain; Which the Party which is to take the Oath, may Comprehend to be a thing captious and streinable. Their urging Subscription to their own Articles, is but *Lacessere & irritare morbos Ecclesiæ*; Which otherwise would spend themselves: *Non Consensum quærit sed dissidium, qui quod factis præstatur, in verbis exigit. He seeketh not Unity but*

H   *Division,*

Divifion, who exacteth that in words, which we are content to yield in Action.

And it is true, that there are fome, who (I am perfwaded) will not eafily offend by inconformity, who notwithftanding make fome Confcience to fubfcribe : For they know this Note of Inconftancy and Defection from what they have long held, fhall diffable them to do that good, which otherwife they might do. For fuch is the weaknefs of many, that their Miniftry fhould be thereby difcredited *. As for their eafie filencing them in fo great fcarcity of Preachers, it is to *Punifh the People*, and not *Them*. Ought they not (I mean the Bifhops) to keep one eye open, to look upon the good that the men do, but to fix them *both* upon the hurt that they *fuppofe* cometh by them ? Indeed fuch as are *Intemperate and Incorrigible*, God forbid they fhould be permitted to preach: But fhall every inconfiderate word, fomtimes captioufly watched, and for the moft part hardly enforced, be as a forfeiture of their Voice and Gift in preaching ?

* I never metwith any that have forbornfub-fcription on no greater reafon than this.

As for fundry particular moleftations, I take no pleafure to recite them. If a Minifter fhall be troubled for faying in Baptifme (*Do you believe*) for (*Doft thou believe*) If another fhall be call'd in queftion, for praying for her Majefty, without the additions of her Stile. Whereas the very Form of Prayer in the Common-prayer-book hath (*Thy fervant Elizabeth*) and no more : If a third fhall be accufed on thefe words uttered touching the Controverfies, *Tollatur Lex ut fiat certamen,* (whereby was meant that the prejudice of the Law removed, eithers reafons fhould be equally compared) of calling the people to *Sedition* and *Mutiny*, as if he had faid, *Away with the Law, and try it out with Force ;* If thefe and other like particulars be true, which I have

but

but by Rumor, and cannot affirm; *it is* to be lamented that they ſhould labour among us with ſo little Comfort—The wrath of man worketh not the Righteouſneſs of God.

Thus far this conformable Learned Lawyer.

The ſaid Lord Verulam *in his* Conſiderations for the better Pacification and Edification of the Church of *England, Pag.* 180. &c. of his Works.

He firſt anſwers the Objection that [*It is againſt good Policie to Innovate any thing in Church-matters :* And praiſing the Church, addeth, *pag.* 182. *But for the Diſcipline and Orders of the Church; as many, and the Chief of them, are Holy and Good; ſo yet if Saint* John *were to indite an Epiſtle to the Church of* England, *as he did to them of* Aſia, *it would ſure have the Clauſe,* Habeo adverſus te pauca.

And he ſaith, pag. 183. *That there ſhould be one Form of Diſcipline in all Churches, and that impoſed by neceſſity of a commandment and preſcript out of the word of God; It is a matter Volumes have been* compiled of, and therefore cannot receive a brief redargution; I for my part do confeſs that in revolving the Scriptures, I could never find any ſuch thing; but that God had left the like liberty to the Church Government, to be varied according to the Time, and Place, and Accidents; which nevertheleſs his high and Divine Providence doth Order and diſpoſe. For all Civil Governments are *reſtrained from God,* unto the *General Grounds* of *Juſtice and Manners.* But the *Policies* and *Forms* of them are left free; So that Monarchies and Kingdoms, Senates and Seigniories, Popular States and Communalties, are lawful; and

where

where they are planted ought to be maintained inviolate.

So likewise in *Church* matters, the *Substance of Doctrine* is *immutable* : And so are the *General Rules* of *Government* : But for *Rites* and *Ceremonies*, and for the *particular Hierarchies*, *Policies*, and *Discipline* of Churches, they be left at large.

And therefore it is good that we *return to the ancient bounds of Unity* in the *Church of God* : which was, *One Faith*, *One Baptism* ; and not *One Hierarchy,One Discipline* : And that we observe the *League of Christians* as it is penned by our *Saviour* ; which is, in *substance of Doctrine* this, [*He that is not with us is against us.*] But in things *Indifferent* and of *Circumstance*, this [*He that is not against us is with us.*]

In these things, so as the General rule be observed, [*That Chrifts flock be fed: That there be a succession in Bishops and Ministers, which are* the *Prophets* of the *New Testament* ; *That there be a due and reverent use of the Power of the Keyes* ; *That thofe that preach* the *Gofpel, live of the Gofpel* ; *That all things tend to Edification* ; *That all things be done in order, and with decency*, and the like,] The rest is left to Holy Wifdom,and fpiritual difcretion of the Mafter-Builder, and Inferior Builders in Chrifts Church. As it is excellently alluded by that Father that noted that Chrifts Garment was without Seam ; and yet the Churches Garment was of divers Colours: And fetsdown as a rule : *In vefte varietas fit* ; *fciffura non fit.*

Pag. 134. For the Government of Bifhops, I for my part, not prejudging the Prefidents of other reformed Churches, do hold it *warranted* by the Word of God, and by the Practice of the ancient Church in the better times ; and much more Convenient for Kingdoms than *Parity* of Minifters, and Government by Synods. But there

be

be two Circumſtances in the Adminiſtration of Biſhops; wherein I confeſs I could never be ſatisfyed: The One, *The ſole exerciſe of their Authority* : The other, The *Deputation* of their Authority.

For the firſt, The Biſhop giveth *Orders-alone, Excommunicateth alone, Judgeth alone:* This ſeemeth to be a thing almoſt without Example in good Government, and therefore not unlikely to have crept in in the degenerate and corrupt time: We ſee the greateſt Kings and Monarchs have their Councils: There is no Temporal Court in *England* of the higher ſort, where the Authority doth reſt in one perſon. The Kings-Bench, the Common-pleas, and the Exchequer, are Benches of a certain Number of Judges. The Chancellor of *England*, hath the Aſſiſtance of twelve Maſters of the *Chancery.* &c. The like is to be found in all well-govern'd Commonwealths abroad, where the Juriſdiction is more diſperſed : As in the Court of Parliament of *France*, and in other places.

No man will deny, but the Acts that paſſe the Biſhops Juriſdiction, are of as great importance as thoſe that paſs the Civil Courts : For mens Souls are more precious than their Bodies or Goods: And ſo are their Good-names : Biſhops have their infirmities ; and have no exception from that general Malediction, pronounced againſt all Men living : *Væ Soli, nam ſi occident*, &c. Nay we ſee that the firſt Warrant in Spiritual Cauſes is directed to a *Number*, *Dic Eccleſiæ*, which is not ſo in Temporal Matters, *Ab initio non fuit ſic.*

For the ſecond Point, which is the *Deputation of their Authority*, I ſee no perfect nor ſure ground for that neither. Being ſomewhat different from the Examples and Rules of Government. The Biſhop exerciſeth his Juriſdiction by his Chancellour and Commiſſary, Official, &c. We ſee in all Laws in the world, *Offices of Confidence* and *Skill* cannot:

not be put over and exercifed by Deputy, except it be fpecially contained in the Original Grant. And in that Cafe it is dutiful. And for experience, there was never any Chancellour of *England* made a Deputy : There was never any Judge in any Court made a Deputy: The Bifhop is a Judge, and of a high nature : whence cometh it that he fhould depute ? Confidering that all Truft and Confidence is perfonal and inherent ; and cannot, nor ought not be tranfpofed. Surely in this again *Ab initio non fuit fic.* But it is probable, that Bifhops when they gave themfelves too much to the glory of the world, and became Grandees in Kingdoms, and great Counfellours to Princes, then did they delegate their proper Jurifdictions, as things of too inferior Nature for their Greatnefs; And then after the fimilitude of Kings and Count Palatines, they would have their Chancellours and Judges.

But the Example of Kings and Potentates giveth no good defence: For the Reafon why Kings adminifter by their Judges, tho' themfelves are fupream Judges, are two: The One, becaufe the Offices of Kings are for the moft part of Inheritance. And it is a Rule in all Laws, that offices of inheritance, are rather matters that ground in Intereft than in Confidence, for as much as they may fall upon Women, upon Infants, upon Lunaticks and Idiots, Perfons uncapable to execute Judicature in perfon. And therefore fuch Offices, by all Laws, might ever be exercifed and adminiftred by delegation. The fecond reafon is, becaufe of the Amplitude of their Jurifdictions, &c. There is a third reafon, tho' not much to the prefent purpofe, that Kings, either in refpect of the Common-wealth, or of the Greatnefs of their own Patrimonies, are ufually Parties in Suites : And then their Judges ftand indifferent between them and their Subjects. But in the Cafe of Bifhops none of thefe Reafons hold : For firft, their Office

is

el e ctive and for life, and not patrimonial or heredi-
tary: An Office meerly of *Confidence*, *Science*, and *Qua-
lification*, &c. *See the rest.*

Page. 185, 186. The Cap and Surplice since they be
things in their Nature indifferent, and yet by some held
Superstitious, and that the Question is between *Science*
and *Conscience*, it seemeth to fall within the compass of the
Apostles Rule, which is, that the stronger do descend and
yield to the weaker, &c. [*lege cætera*] The rather because
the silencing of Ministers on this occasion, is in this
scarcity of good Preachers, a punishment that lighteth on
the people, as well as on the party.

And for the *Subscription*, it seemeth to me in the Nature
of a Confession, and therefore more proper to bind in the
Unity of Faith, and to be urged rather for *Articles of Doctrine*, than for *Rites* and *Ceremonies*, and Points of *outward
Government*. For howsoever publick Considerations and Reasons of State may require Uniformity, yet *Christian and
Divine Grounds* look chiefly upon Unity.

See what he saith *pag.*191. for A. Bishop *Grindals* way of
Lectures to young Ministers, to teach them to preach well.
And *p.* 192 of the abuse of Excommunication.

An Animadversion of the Transcriber.

Qu. *Why was this great man so much against Bishops depu-
ting their proper work to Chancellours, Commissaries, Offici-
als ?* &c.

Ans. It's easie to conjecture,

I. Tho' he thought the accidental Modes of Church-Government mutable and humane, yet most Christians with
him judge, that the *Essentials* of *Church Office* are of Divine Institution, and therefore fixed on the proper Officers:
And that no Lay-man may by Deputation administer Sacraments, or the Church Keyes. II. And

II. And so he would not have Lay-men and the Clergie confounded, as if there were nothing proper to the Pastoral Office, left it teach the Laity Sacrilegious Usurpation. The *Office* is nothing but a conjunction of *Obligation* and *Authority* to do the *works:* And if a Lay-man have these two, he is a Bishop.

III. The very confounding of the *Bishops Office* and the *Presbyters*, seemeth so ill to many, that they think even a Presbyter (Archdeacon or Chancellor) may not be deputed to the work of the Bishop, because that maketh him a Bishop, much less may a Lay-man. ·

IV. Many would not have the *King or Civil Magistrate* made properly a Bishop, and so the Offices Confounded : But say they, If *commissioning* another to Judge by the Keyes, or to administer Sacraments, be proper to a Bishop, then Kings and Magistrates are Bishops; for they may send and Commission other men to do all this.

V. The *Bishops personal doing of all his own proper Office-works,* would answer almost all that the moderate Nonconformists desire in Church Government : For then,

1. The Keyes we hope would be used in a Sacred serious manner, with due Admonition, Instruction, Exhortation, Prayer, &c. which might melt a Sinner into Repentance.

2. And then Experience would fully satisfie the Diocesans that they *must needs have Bishops under* them, or besides them, at least in every great Town, with the adjoining Parishes : For by that time they had duely *Confirmed all* before *Communicating*, and had *examined*, exhorted, and *judged the many* hundred Scandalous Persons that in a Diocess would be presented, I'le warrant you they would be glad of the help of many : And though perhaps Church-Wardens would not present all that come not to Church, in the Parishes where many Score thousands keep away

for

for want of room, or on that pretence ; yet good Minifters would prefent more than now they do, when
they faw it would tend to a facred ufe of the
Keyes, and mens repentance. *Bucer's* defire of Parifh
Difcipline, would be fure more performed, which would
end moft Church Controverfies,

VI. And this would bring in many Nonconformifts,
who now ftand out, becaufe they dare not make *a Covenant, an Oath,* never in their *places to endeavour any alteration of Church Government,* becaufe they think *Lay
Chancellours ufe of the Keyes decretively unlawful.* And
dare not fwear Obedience to fuch Ordinances ; nor yet
own the Omiffion of Difcipline which the paucity of
Bifhops unavoidably inferreth, while a Diocefs hath
but one. (Experience would certainly cure that).

VII. And it moveth fome, that we yet meet with
few Bifhops that will defend lay Chancellours decretive
ufe of the Keyes ; but feem to wifh it were reformed.

VIII. And the Chancellours and Civilians have little
reafon to be offended with my Lord *Verulam,* and fuch
men : For he would allow them the probate of Wills,
and Matrimonial Cafes, and all that belongeth to an
Official Magiftrate, that hath his Office from the King.
And no doubt would confent that they have a moderate Power by mulcts to conftrain men to fubmit to
their Courts, inftead of the ufe of Excommunications
and Abfolutions,

They fay this is otherwife in *Scotland* now. And
yet they are fworn not to endeavour any alteration of
Church Government.

And I hope none will be angry with this Learned
great man, for the blame which he layeth on the Bifhops ufage of the Non-Conformifts ; even before the

I   prefent

prefent Canons were made: Since, 1. His Letters fhew him to have been a man extraordinarily humbling himfelf both to the Queen and to the Bifhops. 2. And the moſt approved Hiſtorians tell us, to our great grief, that fuch things have been no wonders and rarities, thefe thirteen hundred years. It is holy and credible men that tell us, how St. *Martin*, notwithſtanding all his Miracles and holinefs, was ufed by the *Synods* of Biſhops in his time, for being fo ſtrict of life, and fo much againſt the ufing of the Sword againſt the *Prifcilian Gnoſtick* Hereticks.

And it is as holy and credible men that tell us how St. *Theophilus Alexander*, a Patriarch, envyed and ufed his Superior Patriarch, holy *Chryfoſtome*, and even long ſtudied his ruine: And how another called St. *Epiphanius*, feditiouſly came out of *Cyprus*, and affronted him at *Conſtantinople*, in his own Church, requiring him irregularly before all the People, to Curfe *Origen* or his Writings; as if the Biſhop of the *Iſle of Man* ſhould come and magiſterially impofe this on the Biſhop of *London* or *Canterbury*, in the Congregation where he preach'd. They tell us how readily the Synods of Biſhops Condemned *Chryfoſtome*, becaufe the Emperour and Emprefs were againſt him: And if fo excellent and holy a man, whofe language and life excelled them all, could not efcape condemnation twice over, and that in the Age of the Church which is predicated for the very beſt and happieſt that ever was fince the days of Chriſt; If the Primacy among all the four Eaſtern Patriarchs, and his own rare Parts, and holinefs and innocency, could not fecure him from ejection and baniſhment from a famous Chriſtian Emperour, and the Convocations of Biſhops that envyed his holinefs and parts; If when he was baniſhed, his ſtable conſtant flock, that would not renounce

nounce him, were made Conventiclers, and named *Joannits*, as a note of Schifmatical Separatifts, while thofe that turned to the next poffeffour were called the Church. If another Saint of greateft Learning, Name and Power, refifted the very reftoring of his name when he was dead, faying the Canons were not to be broken to fatisfie the Schifmatical *Joannits*, whom nothing will fatisfie, and that it would difcourage the Conformifts; I mean St. *Cyril* of *Alexandria*; why fhould it be thought that men far inferiour to *Chryfoftome*, that live not in fo pure an Age, fhould by the Clergie ftream and power, be much like efteemed, and partly ufed.

And if in thofe Ages of the Churches greateft excellency (the 4*th*. and 5*th*. Centuries) the great Patriarchs themfelves of *Alexandria*, *Antioch*, *Conftantinople*, &c. who are fuppofed by fome to be the Pillars of the Church for Government and Unity, did live almoft in continual Conflict, Curfing, or cafting out each other as Hereticks, or Schifmaticks, and oft fighting it out in Chriftian blood, (to fay nothing of the following worfer Ages) what wonder, if ftill the old Caufes fucceeding produce many of the old Effects: Which a man that was thought wife enough to be the Lord Chancellour of *England*, and the famous reftorer of Learning, might be allowed gently to touch, while the Clergy themfelves openly and greatly prefer thofe Ages, and the *Theophilus's*, *Epiphanius's*, and *Cyrils*, and Epifcopal Synods thereof, before our own, and before themfelves.

Let us hear what one more excellent perfon, and no Fanatick or Schifmatick faith.

Dr. *Ifaack Barrow* (a man, if ever this Age had any, that delivered *digefted TRUTH* in *clear Expreffions*) vol. 2. *p*. 34.

" Whoever indeed will confider the Nature of man,

or

" or will confult obvious experience, fhall find that in
" practical matters, our *will* or *appetite* hath a mighty in-
" fluence on our *Judgment* of things, caufing men with
" great attention to regard that which they affect, and
" carefully to mark all reafons making for it; but a-
" verting from that which they diflike, and making them
" to overlook the arguments which perfwade it : whence
" men generally do fuit their opinions to their inclina-
" tions;   warping to that fide where their *INTEREST*
" doth lye; or to which their Complexions, their Humor,
" their Paffions, their Pleafure, their eafe doth fway them;
" So that almoft any Notion will feem true, which is
" *Profitable*, which is *Safe*, which is *Pleafant*, or any way
" grateful to them; and that Notion *falfe*, which in any fuch
" refpect doth crofs them. Very few can abftract their
" minds from fuch confiderations, or embrace *Pure Truth*
" divefted of them. And thofe few who do fo, muft therein
" moft employ their *Will*, by ftrong effects of Voluntary
" refolution, and patience, and difengaging their minds
" from thofe clogs and byaffes.

   " This is particularly notorious in mens adhering to
" *Parties*, divided in opinion, which is fo regulated by
" that fort of caufes, that if you do mark what any mans
" *Temper* is, and where his *INTEREST* lyeth, you may
" eafily prognofticate on what fide he will be; and with
" what degree of Serioufnefs, of Vigour, of Zeal, he will
" cleave thereto. A timerous man you may be almoft
" fure will be on the *fafer* fide : A *Covetous* man will bend
" to that Party where *Gain* is to be had. An *Ambitious*
" man will clofe with the opinion paffing in *Court*. A
" *carelefs* man will comply with the *fafhion*: Affection ari-
" fing from *Education* or *Prejudice* will hold others ftiff.
" Few follow the refults of *Impartial Contemplation*.

   And *pag.* 483. " There is one Lawgiver who can fave
                                                       and

" and deftroy : *Who art thou that Judgeft another?* That is,
" How intollerably Rafh, Unjuft and arrogant art thou,
" who fetteft thy felf on Gods Tribunal, and thence doft ad-
" venture to pronounce Doom upon his People? Did we
" well confider Gods Judgment, we fhould rather think it
" advifeable to be mindful of our own Cafe, than to pafs
" Sentence on that of others: Obferving how lyable our
" felves are, we fhould fcarce have a Heart to Carp at o-
" thers; finding what great need our actions will then have
" of a Favourable Interpretation, we fhould fure be more
" candid and mild in Cenfuring other mens Actions: Special-
" ly confidering, that by harfh Judgment of others, we
" make our own Cafe worfe, and inflame our reckoning:
" We directly thence incur Guilt, we aggravate our own
" Offences, and render our felves unexcufable; we expofe our
" felves on that fcore to Condemnation. See *Mat.* 7. 2. *Luk.*
6. 37. *Rom.* 2. 2, 3. *Jam.* 5. 9.

His two Sermons on *Ro.* 12. 18. well practifed, would
heal *England's* Divifions.

Such alfo is his Sermon of Love to our Neighbour,
that againft Slander, and that againft Detraction : But that
which I cite him for, is the very fame defcription of Religion which Judge *Hale* giveth. *Serm.* 1. p. 10.

" The Principal advantage of Wifdom, is its acquain-
" ting us with the Nature and Reafon of true Religion,
" and affording Convictive Arguments to perfwade the
" Practice of it: Which is accompanied with the pureft de-
" light, and attended with the moft folid content imagina-
" nable: I fay, the Nature of Religion, wherein it Confifts, and
" what it requires : The miftake of which produceth daily
" fo many mifchiefs and inconveniences in the World, and
" expofeth fo good a Name to fo much Reproach. It fhew-
" eth it confifteth not in fair profeffions and glorious pre-
tences,

" tences, but in Real Practice ; not in a pertinacious ad-
" herence to ANY Sect, or Party, but in a sincere Love of
" Goodness, and dislike of Naughtiness wherever discove-
" ring it self; not in Vain Ostentations and Flourishes of
" outward performance, but in an inward good complexi-
" on of Mind, exerting it self in Works of true *Devotion*
" and *Charity*, not in a Nice Orthodoxie, or *Politick*
" *Subjection* of our Judgments to the peremptory
" dictates of Men ; but in a sincere Love of Truth, and hear-
" ty approbation and compliance with the Doctrines *Funda-*
" *mentally Good* and *Necessary* to be believed : Not in harsh
" censuring and virulently inveighing against others, but
" in careful amending our own ways : Not in a peevish
" crossness and obstinate Repugnancy to received Laws and
" Customs; but in a quiet and Peaceable Submission to the
" express Laws of God, and Lawful Commands of Men :
" Not in a furious Zeal FOR or AGAINST trivial Circum-
" stances, but in a conscionable practising the substantial
" parts of Religion : Not in a frequent talking, or contenti-
" ous disputing about it ; but in a ready observance of the
" unquestionable Rules and Precepts of it. In a Word, True
" Religion consists in nothing else, but doing what becomes
" our Relation to God, in a Conformity or similitude to his
" Nature, and in a willing Obedience to his Holy Will, to
" which by potent incentives it allures and perswades us, by
" representing to us his transcendent glorious Attributes—
" &c. *See the rest, too long to be transcribed.*

If you say, *A Papist will own all this.* I answer, 1. So
much the better : We will not feign a new Christianity
to differ from Papists. 2. But do they not own too much
more ? How then come they to fill the World with Blood
and Division, for the Sake of their numerous humane
Additionals ?

I know

I know no man that hath more fully confuted that Sect than he hath done in his *Treatise of Supremacy and Church-Unity*: And saith the Publisher of his Life, [*He understood Popery both at home and abroad. He had narrowly observed it Militant in* England, *triumphant in* Italy, *disguised in* France; *and had earlier apprehensions of the Approaching Danger, and would have appeared with the forwardest in a needful time.*

Whoever will truly confute his Treatise of the *Popes Supremacy*, and that of the *Unity of the Church*, against the Supremacy and Foreign Jurisdiction of Councils called General, I here promise him shall make me a Papist (of the Italian.or the Gallicane sort accordingly) if he will do it before I die, and am Disabled from reading and considering it. But I doubt not but the Papists will rather study to bury it in silence, (while they do their works by other means than Reasoning) lest the notice of a Confutation should occasion more to read it: And then, especially if all men in Power should read it, their Cause with such is utterly undone.

Saith Dr. *Tillotson* in his Preface to it, [*I dare say that whoever shall carefully peruse this Treatise, will find that this point of the Popes Supremacy (on which* Bellarmine *hath the confidence to say, The whole of* Christianity *depends) is not only an indefensible, but an Impudent Cause, as ever was undertaken by learned Pens: And nothing could have kept it so long from becoming ridiculous in the judgment of Mankind, but its being so strongly supported by a worldly interest: For there is not one tolerable argument for it,* and *there are a thousand invincible Reasons against it.*

If

IF thefe three Teftimonies of the moft Learned, Wife, and Impartial Conformifts, that thefe (or many) Ages have bred, be all born down by Intereft and Supercilious Confidence, and a Flood of Words (which may all be u-fed for the worft Caufe in the World) the Lord be Judge, and juftifie his Truth, and that Wifdom from above, *Jam.* 3. 17. which is juftified of her Children. When Satan hath done his worft, *Bleffed are the Peace-makers ; for they fhall be called the Children of God.* Mat. 5. 9.

Read Nov. 8. 1697.
April. 1. 1709.

FINIS.